# PADDLE
# THE NORTH OF ENGLAND

The Best Places to Go with a
Paddleboard, Kayak or Canoe

BRUCE SMITH

ADLARD COLES
Bloomsbury Publishing Plc
50 Bedford Square, London, WC1B 3DP, UK
Bloomsbury Publishing Ireland Limited,
29 Earlsfort Terrace, Dublin 2, D02 AY28, Ireland

BLOOMSBURY, ADLARD COLES and the Adlard Coles logo are
trademarks of Bloomsbury Publishing Plc

First published in Great Britain 2026

A catalogue record for this book is available from the
British Library

Library of Congress Cataloguing-in-Publication data has
been applied for

ISBN: PB: 978-1-3994-2183-6; ePub: 978-1-3994-2180-5;
ePDF: 978-1-3994-2182-9

2 4 6 8 10 9 7 5 3 1

Art editor Louise Turpin
Set in Frutiger
Printed and bound in China by Toppan
Leefung

To find out more about our authors and
books visit www.bloomsbury.com and sign
up for our newsletters

For product safety related questions contact
productsafety@bloomsbury.com

FSC
www.fsc.org
MIX
Paper | Supporting
responsible forestry
FSC® C104723

## IMPORTANT SAFETY NOTICE AND LEGAL DISCLAIMER

# PADDLE
# THE NORTH OF ENGLAND

## The Best Places to Go with a Paddleboard, Kayak or Canoe

### BRUCE SMITH

ADLARD
COLES

LONDON · OXFORD · NEW YORK · NEW DELHI · SYDNEY

# CONTENTS

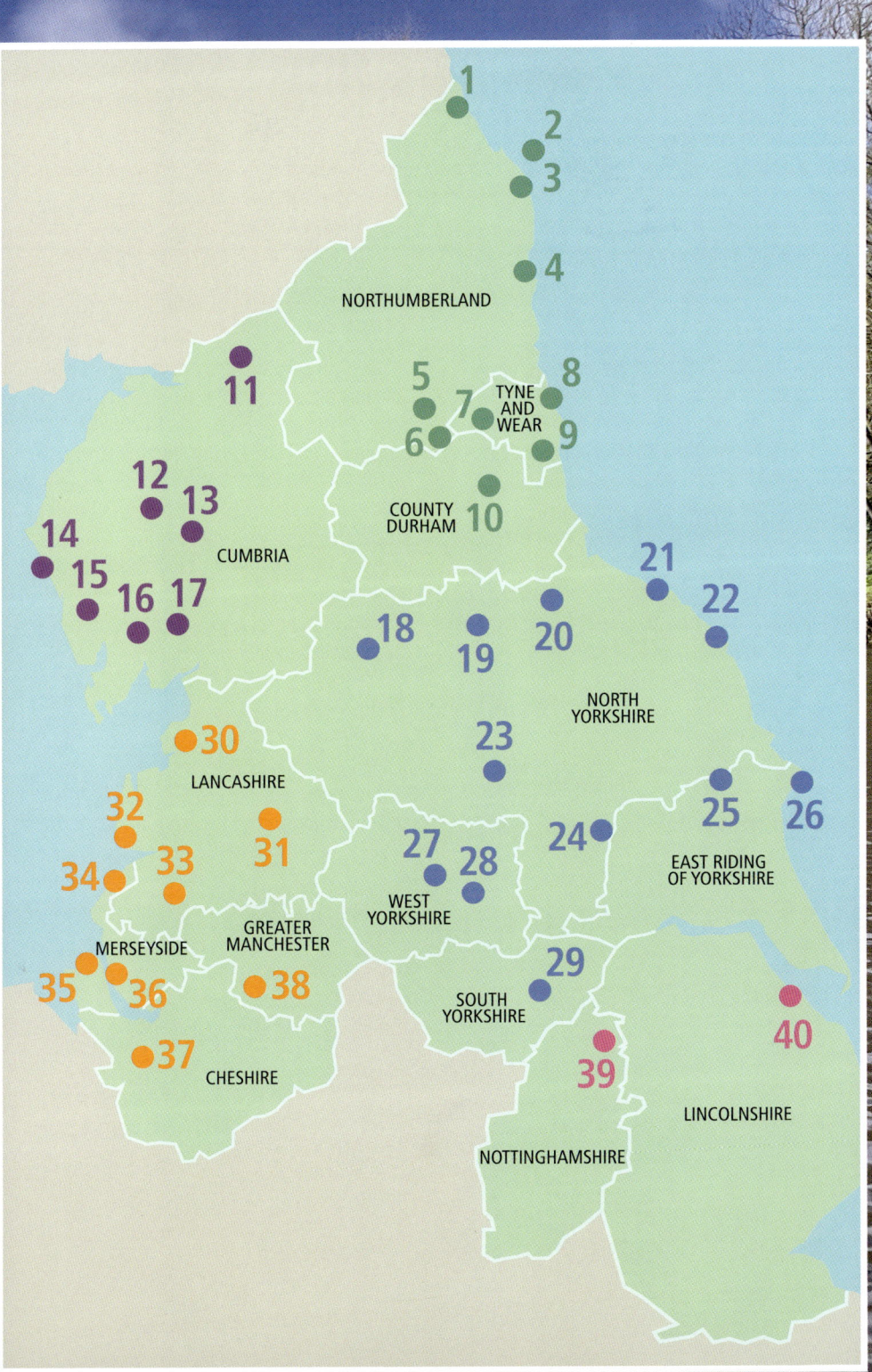

# INTRODUCTION

*'Once upon a time, not so very many years ago, it was possible to travel all over England, north, south, east and west, by river and canal; there was not a county you could not visit, hardly a town you could not reach by water, if you liked and if you were not (and what lover of boats and rivers ever was or will be?) in any particular hurry to get there.'*

William Bliss, *The Heart of England by Waterway* (1933)

Come along and join me on an incredible journey as I explore the very best the North of England has to offer. Whether you're a seasoned paddler or a novice discovering the joys of paddling for the first time, the North of England promises unforgettable experiences. From picturesque lakes and winding rivers to tranquil canals and dramatic coastal areas, the North of England is a true paddlers' paradise. Explore the stunning landscapes of Cumbria's Lake District, the breathtaking beauty of the Yorkshire Dales or the rugged charm of Northumberland's coastline. Whether it's a short, playful paddle or a full-day expedition, you'll discover historic sites and encounter nature at its finest.

Featuring 40 different routes, this book covers popular paddles and hidden gems across the North East, the North West, Cumbria, Yorkshire, Humberside and North Lincolnshire.

Featuring beautiful photography and clear maps, this is the ultimate guide to explore and see the very best of Northern England under paddle power. Discover where to go, how to get there, and how you can make the most of your trip.

## Biodiversity and Paddling: Protecting Our Waterways

Biodiversity refers to the variety of life in an environment, including plants, animals

and micro-organisms. Healthy rivers, lakes and coastal waters support a rich mix of species, from fish and aquatic plants to birds and insects. These ecosystems rely on a delicate balance, and paddlers have a responsibility to help protect them.

One of the biggest threats to biodiversity in waterways is the spread of invasive species – non-native plants and animals that disrupt the natural ecosystem. These species often outcompete native wildlife, clog up rivers and damage habitats. As paddlers, we can unknowingly transport invasive species from one waterway to another on our boats, paddles or gear. To help prevent this, follow the Check, Clean, Dry approach:

- Check your boat or board, paddle and gear for any plant matter, mud or small creatures before leaving for home.
- Clean everything thoroughly with fresh water, paying special attention to hidden areas where invasive species may cling.
- Dry your equipment completely before using it in a different body of water, as some invasive species can survive for long periods of time in damp conditions.

## About the Author

Bruce Smith is a British Stand Up Paddle Association (BSUPA) instructor and co-founder of Northern SUP Race Team. A Naish SUP ambassador, Bruce is a highly experienced paddleboarder who has as much passion for helping complete beginners learn new skills as he does for racing his Naish Javelin in national and international competitions.

After a debilitating ankle injury that would prevent him running ever again, Bruce was at a loss; his ability to compete in Ironman and ultra-marathon races was the 'medicine' needed to battle Post Traumatic Stress Disorder and pull him out of a dark place. After learning he would no longer be able to run, thankfully he found Stand Up Paddle (SUP). It continues to be a positive influence on his life and he hasn't looked back!

Bruce lives with his partner, Karen, in Consett, the town he grew up in. His love for the water developed from spending school holidays playing in the surf at Bamburgh beach on England's north-east coast, which remains to this day one of his favourite paddle locations.

BELOW Dan Smith taking in the views of Bamburgh Castle.

## What to wear

Along with most sports, what to wear for paddleboarding mainly comes down to personal choice, budget, type of craft you are paddling and the conditions you are going out in. Here, I will go through some suggestions on what is available, based on my own experiences and what I've learned along my own paddle journey, and aim to break down the minefield of clothing and equipment.

One of the best pieces of advice I can give concerns the weather you encounter on the water, which can be unpredictable. I'm sure many of us have experienced this: one moment you're enjoying a nice leisurely paddle in the sunshine, and the next minute a squall sweeps through. The water chops up, the rain starts falling and before you know it, you're soaked to the skin and getting cold fast. While this simple guide can't control the changing conditions, it will help you be prepared for whatever the weather throws at you. It's by no means a definitive list of must-haves as we are all different, with different needs, and what works for one person may not be suitable for another.

I've separated this guide into five main topics: base layers; top layers; wetsuits; drysuits; and head, hands and feet.

### Base layers

Base layers are the foundation of a layer system. Ideally designed to be worn next to the skin, they play a key role in keeping you comfortable while paddling, helping to manage moisture and regulate body temperature. They should be comfortable to wear and have good moisture-wicking capabilities; this helps draw sweat away from the skin and keeps you dry. Base layers are also excellent for preventing chaffing from wetsuits or buoyancy aids.

You can buy watersport-specific base layers and rash vests, which are an excellent choice if you're wearing a wetsuit. A merino-wool base layer is also a great option under a wetsuit or drysuit, as it

retains its insulating properties even when wet – perfect for situations where water might seep into your suit. Over the years, I have spent a fortune on expensive base layers, but if I'm honest, some of the best ones I use on the water these days are budget options from discount high-street stores. I originally bought them to keep me warm while climbing communications towers at work during the winter, as the layering system works really well when I'm moving around a transmission tower 300ft above ground. They've proven just as effective for paddling.

Base layers are not just for wearing under wetsuits and drysuits. It's always worth taking one with you in a dry bag as you can soon cool down while stopping for a picnic or if the sun disappears behind the clouds.

## Top layers
Even when paddling in summer, it's wise to carry an extra top layer in a dry bag; if you stop paddling even for a short time, you can cool down quickly. Windproof tops are an excellent choice – they're lightweight and effective at blocking the wind, helping you stay warm even on cooler days. I always pack my old trusty windproof running jacket, a bargain find from a charity shop, just in case. A sailing cag, also called a cagoule, is also a good option and the rubber hem helps it resist riding up while you're paddling. For the lower body, windproof and waterproof running trousers are easy to slip on over boots and very comfortable to paddle in. Try to avoid tops and bottoms with lots of pockets and zips. These can be quite cumbersome and a hindrance if you need to self-rescue. At worst, they may even become an entrapment hazard.

LEFT Sup Yoga at Ellerton Lake (credit Daniel Godridge).

BELOW Geared up for an expedition on the River Derwent.

**Wetsuits** Wetsuits come in many shapes and sizes. Typically made from neoprene, they work by trapping a thin layer of water between your skin and the suit, and this water is warmed by your body heat, providing a layer of insulation. They generally range in thickness from 2mm to 5mm or feature a combination of thicknesses, which can benefit paddlers by offering more flexibility around the shoulders. Long John or Long Jane suits are particularly popular with paddlers due to their sleeveless, vest-style tops, which allow for unrestrictive shoulder movement.

When choosing a wetsuit, fit is crucial. A snug fit prevents water from flushing through, but it shouldn't be so tight that it restricts your movement or breathing. It's also worth noting that wetsuits can have zips at the front, back or shoulders. While this might seem like a minor detail, it can become a real challenge – like the time I found myself hopping around a car park, struggling to locate the zip cord at the back, only to end up asking a stranger to help zip it up!

Prices for wetsuits can vary dramatically, and in my experience the more you pay, the better the quality in terms of warmth and flexibility. However, over the years I've found myself only wearing a full wetsuit when paddling in choppy seas or surfing the waves. For flatter water, I prefer a pair of neoprene trousers combined with a base layer and windproof cag. This set-up allows me to adjust layers as needed and I find it much more comfortable than a full wetsuit.

**Drysuits** There are almost as many options for drysuits as there are for wetsuits. Overall, they are designed to keep you dry; however, some are classed as semi-dry wetsuits, and these have tight neoprene cuffs at the feet that enable you to wear your usual footwear. Others have waterproof socks stitched into them – these do require looking after to prevent damage. Never walk around on hard ground without overshoes as they are easily pierced. You can get one-piece and two-piece suits, and they can vary dramatically in materials used, from extra lightweight racing suits to full thick suits more tailored to leisure and cruising paddles.

RIGHT Paddling along the Bridgewater Canal into Manchester.

BELOW An autumn paddle on the lake.

## Head, hands and feet

Keeping your extremities warm in colder temperatures can be crucial to the enjoyment of paddling throughout the winter months. However, cold weather isn't the only reason to consider wearing hats, gloves and boots. They can also be valuable in protecting from the sun's rays and gloves can help prevent blisters on longer paddles.

### Headwear

Beanies, woolly hats or balaclavas are excellent for keeping you warm, while caps and bucket hats are great for protecting your head from the sun. Personally, I like to wear a moisture-wicked snood – it's the most versatile piece of clothing a paddler can carry. Practical and adaptable, it can be worn on the head or neck in various ways and can easily be wrapped around the wrist when not needed.

### Hands

Keeping your hands warm and comfortable while paddling can be tricky. Neoprene gloves are effective at keeping your hands warm but they can be big, stiff and cumbersome. This can cause discomfort and, for some, even lead to aches in the forearms. It's a good idea to try neoprene gloves on before buying.

An alternative option is palmless mitts, which combine the warmth of neoprene with an open-palm design that allows a better connection to the paddle. Over the years, I have tried so many other options including walking gloves, gym gloves and mountain bike gloves. However, I've found myself consistently using nitrile general-purpose work gloves. They are inexpensive, durable and while not quite as warm as neoprene, they do help block the wind and wind chill while letting me feel the paddle.

For kayakers, another great option is 'pogies'. These mitts attach directly to the paddle and are fantastic for keeping the hands warm and dry.

### Feet

Once again, there are plenty of options for footwear, ranging from split-toe surfing booties and basic neoprene boots to specialised kayak boots or SUP-specific shoes. You don't have to spend a lot of money: simple water shoes or even everyday trainers can work just as well. For added warmth, thermal, waterproof or neoprene socks are an excellent choice to wear under boots. One of the joys of SUP paddling is going barefoot – there's nothing quite like the feeling of warm water washing over your feet as you glide along. However, it is always advisable to carry some form of footwear that you can easily slip on for portaging or accessing and exiting the water.

# Equipment

## Boats and boards

The options for paddle craft are almost limitless – whether you're surfing waves, navigating white water or cruising on an expedition, there's something for everyone. While most craft can handle a variety of activities, choosing one tailored more towards your needs will enhance your paddling experience.

## Size and shape

The length of your board or boat significantly impacts its handling. Longer boards glide better. They also track straighter, making them ideal for touring and covering longer distances. However, they can be more challenging to turn. Shorter boards, on the other hand, are much easier to manoeuvre but with the trade-off of being slower. This can lead to zigzagging along as opposed to smooth gliding.

The width of the paddle craft affects its stability and speed – wider craft offer more stability, making them great for beginners or heavier paddlers, while narrower ones are faster but less stable.

The construction of your craft is another important consideration. For SUPs you have two options, hard boards and inflatables. Hard boards, typically made of carbon fibre or fibreglass, are firmer, provide better glide and generally offer a more enjoyable paddling experience. However, they are more fragile so better suited to deep-water, lake and sea paddles. Inflatable boards are softer underfoot and generally

ABOVE Spare kit packed in a drybag (credit Shane Lingford).

more durable, particularly for portages or accessing areas with rocky terrain. They also have the added benefit of being easier to transport and store when not in use. With iSUPs (inflatable stand-up paddleboards), always make sure they are fully inflated. It can be tempting to think it will be OK if it's firm to press in while pumping up. Believe me, if it is just a few psi under the manufacturer's recommendation, it will greatly reduce your paddling experience.

Canoes and kayaks also come in different styles and constructions, each designed for specific needs and environments. Traditional canoes are often made from wood or aluminium, offering durability and classic appeal, while modern models utilise materials like fibreglass, Kevlar or carbon fibre for enhanced performance and lighter weight. Similarly, kayaks are available in durable and affordable polyethylene, as well as high-performance composite materials. Inflatable and foldable versions with collapsible frames provide portability with rigidity, making them popular with paddlers with limited storage or seeking convenience.

Fins It is a good idea to have a couple of different fins in your quiver. Changing to a different fin can make a big difference to how your paddleboard performs. The fin height – the vertical distance of the fin from base to tip – determines your stability: the shorter the fin, the less stability you have. A taller fin, while giving extra stability, can be a problem when paddling rivers where there is a risk of grounding out. River fins are much shorter and can be flexible, allowing smoother transition over shallow water, the trade-off being less stability. Another thing to consider is the fin rake – the angle or curvature from base to tip. The curvature also plays a role in control and stability. The more rake the fin has, the better control it has in rougher water, as well as offering easier turning ability. The less the rake, the straighter the fin is – this helps straight-line tracking, but can feel stiffer and harder to turn. It is possible to get balanced fins, which aim to offer the best of both worlds and are great for inexperienced paddlers.

Paddles It would take a whole book to deep-dive into the subject of paddles. They come in an abundance of shapes, sizes and construction materials. There are some things to consider when it comes to buying a paddle, though. It is common for manufacturers of inflatables to sell 'packages' including a paddle. These are cheap, heavy and tend to be made from aluminium and plastic. They are OK for beginners learning the ropes and for short leisurely play paddles, but because of their weight they can be tiring over longer distances. I think it is always a good idea, if budget allows, to upgrade to a lighter paddle. It is also important to choose a blade size that suits your body size: generally, a smaller, lighter paddler will need a smaller blade size. If the blade is too small for the paddler, it can 'slip' rather than 'catch' the water, making it less efficient. SUP paddles also come in adjustable or fixed-length shafts. Fixed-length paddles tend to be lighter and can be more durable due to no moving parts. Adjustable paddles are great for younger paddlers who are still growing. They are also excellent if you are sharing paddles with other people, and for those who use multiple craft and disciplines.

What to take Every paddler is different, with different needs and ideas on what to take while out paddling. If you're unsure, I have compiled a list of ideas to help you pack for your trip:

- Phone in waterproof case
- Personal medication and first-aid kit
- Buoyancy aid
- Waterways licence
- Craft ID sticker with emergency contact details
- Tracker app that automatically raises an alarm should you get into difficulties – Paddle Logger and Garmin Connect are two good options
- Spare clothing
- Food and hydration
- Dry bag or backpack
- Cloths to clean and dry your craft to help prevent cross-contamination of the waterways

## Guide to Safety

**Difficulty rating** All the paddles in this book have been marked with a simple-to-follow difficulty rating. These ratings are based on paddling in good weather, with low wind and normal conditions (that is, rivers not in flood and seas in a calm state). They are a guide for a paddler with a little experience. For people new to paddling, I would advise taking a lesson beforehand and always going out with more experienced paddlers or a guide with local knowledge.

The ratings are:
🔹 **Easy:** Small lake, river in low flow and short distances, beachside paddling
🔹🔹 **Moderate:** Larger lake, faster river, tidal medium distance, tidal estuary
🔹🔹🔹 **Difficult:** Open seas, fast-flowing river water, complex routes

## Paddle safety: Essential tips for a safe trip

Paddling is a fantastic way to explore the water, but safety should always come first. Whether you're on a calm river or open sea, understanding potential hazards and being properly prepared can make all the difference.

**Beware of offshore winds** Winds blowing from the land out to sea – offshore winds – can be deceptively dangerous. They may seem light when launching but will quickly push paddlers away from shore without the paddler realising. It is not until they turn around that they find it difficult to return. Always check the weather forecast before heading out, be aware of wind direction and stay close to shore if in doubt.

**Beware of tides** If you're paddling in coastal water, tides can have a significant impact on your journey. Tidal currents can be strong, especially in narrow channels, and can either speed up your progress or make it extremely difficult. Check tide times and charts before heading out and be mindful that an outgoing tide combined with offshore winds can quickly carry you further from land than expected. Planning your paddle around slack tide (the period between high and low tide, when currents are weaker) can help ensure a safer trip.

**Be able to self-rescue** Even the most skilled paddlers can end up in the water, and knowing how to get back into (or onto) your craft is crucial.

Kayakers should practise wet exits, re-entry techniques, and Eskimo rolls (if using a spray deck).

Canoeists should be familiar with deep water re-entry methods or how to right a capsized boat.

Paddleboarders should practise climbing back on their board from deep water.

Paddle UK (the current governing body for SUP) provide a foundation Paddlesport Safety and Rescue course, which aims to provide paddlers with key safety and rescue skills to help paddlers deal with common problems in sheltered waters.

Leashes There are typically two styles of leashes: straight and coiled. A straight leash is better suited to surfing as there is no spring-back when you fall. For touring or leisure paddling, you don't want the leash dragging in the water behind you; a coiled leash sits nicely on top of the board, eliminating any drag factor. There are many ways to attach the leash to the body, including calf, ankle, waist, with many different attachment types, from Velcro to quick-release systems with ever-changing methods.

The topic of leashes is something that always makes for lively discussion. At the time of writing this book, Paddle UK recommendations can be found on their website – www.paddleuk.org.uk.

Buoyancy aids Also referred to as a personal flotation device (PFD), buoyancy aids buoyancy aids also referred to as a personal flotation device (PFD), are designed to give the wearer flotation should they enter the water. There are many different types of buoyancy aid, each tailored to the specific needs of the activity. According to Paddle UK, a buoyancy aid should comply with CE Standard EN 393 (International Standard – ISO 12402). When choosing a buoyancy aid, it should be bright in colour, the correct size and adjustable. If the buoyancy aid has pockets, zips or straps, ensure they do not impede paddling, self-rescue or exit from your craft.

Some buoyancy aids need to be inflated before use. These are usually small, compact devices attached to the waist and activated by pulling a cord attached to a gas canister. Always make sure you know how to operate these before going out on the water, and carry spare canisters.

Licences I am often asked if you need a licence to paddle on UK waters, and it can lead to interesting conversations. While it's true that people do paddle without a licence or permit – citing reasons like *I didn't know I needed one* or *No one owns water, so why should I have one?* or even *No one ever checks so why should I bother?* – for me, having the appropriate licence is all part and parcel of being a safe and responsible paddler.

While writing this guide, I have been politely questioned on the water several times, so I can confirm: the waterways are most definitely policed. Although enforcement is rare, repeat offence can result in fines of up to £1,000 – enough of a reason for me to renew my membership each year! It's also worth pointing out that the money from licences goes back into maintaining the waterways and improving access to the water for everyone.

The confusion often comes from the fact that not all waterways require a licence or permit. In the Need to Know section of each paddle in this guide, I've noted whether a licence or permit is needed and how to acquire it for that individual paddle.

A Paddle UK membership includes a waterways licence that covers over 4,500km of UK waterways, including those managed by the Canal & River Trust. You can find more information at www.paddleuk.org.uk.

NOTE: All links listed were correct at time of writing. Always check the latest information before heading out on the water.

LEFT When paddling on the coast, check tide times and currents as well as the weather.

## PADDLE UK AND SUP SAFETY

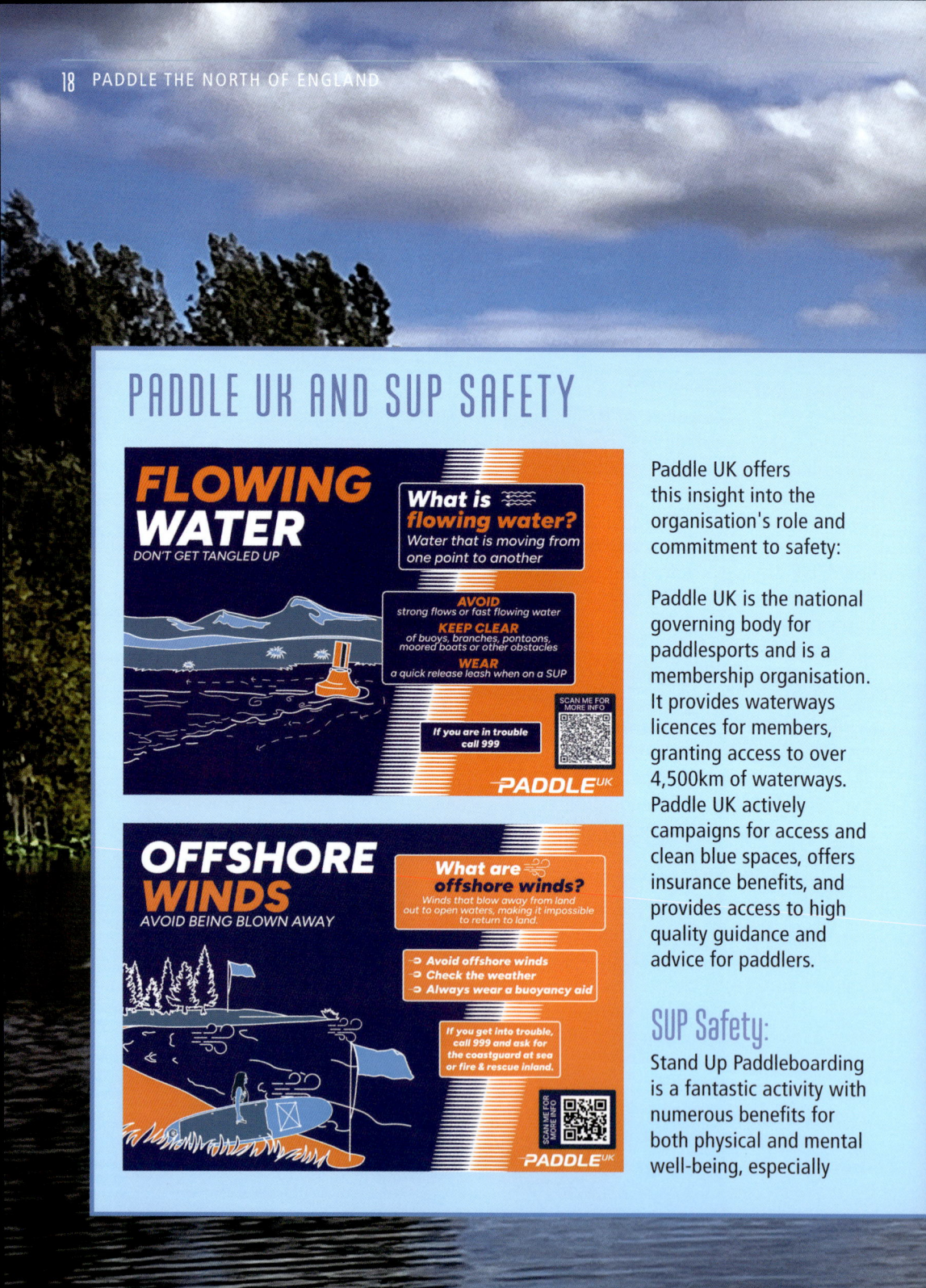

### FLOWING WATER
DON'T GET TANGLED UP

**What is flowing water?**
Water that is moving from one point to another

**AVOID** strong flows or fast flowing water
**KEEP CLEAR** of buoys, branches, pontoons, moored boats or other obstacles
**WEAR** a quick release leash when on a SUP

SCAN ME FOR MORE INFO

If you are in trouble call 999

PADDLE UK

### OFFSHORE WINDS
AVOID BEING BLOWN AWAY

**What are offshore winds?**
Winds that blow away from land out to open waters, making it impossible to return to land.

➡ Avoid offshore winds
➡ Check the weather
➡ Always wear a buoyancy aid

If you get into trouble, call 999 and ask for the coastguard at sea or fire & rescue inland.

SCAN ME FOR MORE INFO

PADDLE UK

Paddle UK offers this insight into the organisation's role and commitment to safety:

Paddle UK is the national governing body for paddlesports and is a membership organisation. It provides waterways licences for members, granting access to over 4,500km of waterways. Paddle UK actively campaigns for access and clean blue spaces, offers insurance benefits, and provides access to high quality guidance and advice for paddlers.

## SUP Safety:

Stand Up Paddleboarding is a fantastic activity with numerous benefits for both physical and mental well-being, especially when enjoyed safely. We always emphasise the following key safety points:

- Always wear a buoyancy aid.
- Use the appropriate leash for the environment (see infographic to the right).
- Carry a mobile phone in a waterproof pouch.
- Check the weather forecast before heading out.
- Inform someone of your planned route and expected return time.
- Know your personal limits and paddle within them.

These graphics created by Paddle UK are a useful summary of the key safety considerations.

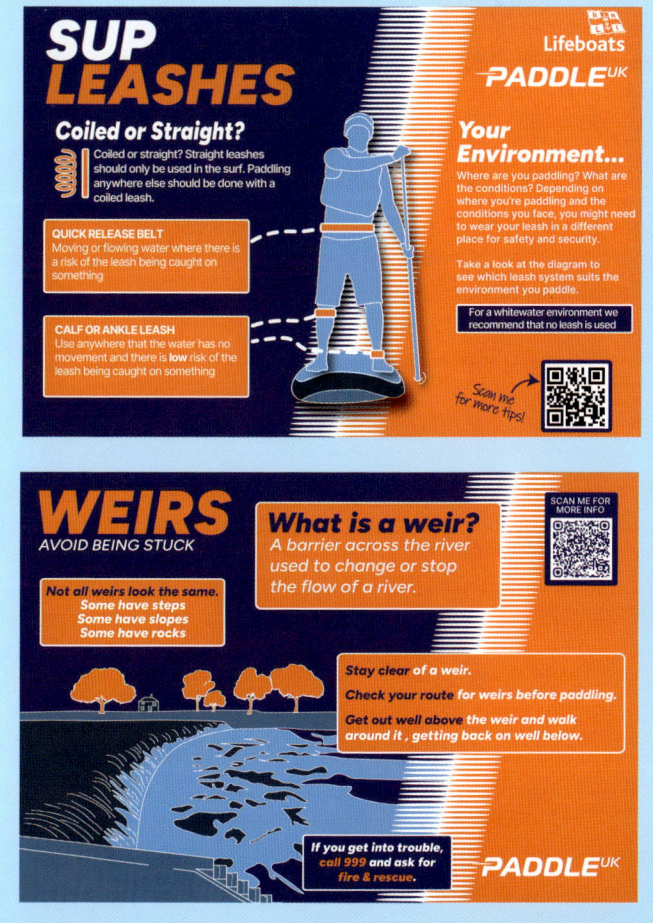

# THE NORTH EAST

The North East of England is a region steeped in history, rich in natural beauty and alive with cultural contrasts. From its rugged coastline and sweeping rural landscapes to its bustling urban centres, this area offers an incredible diversity of experiences for paddlers and adventurers alike.

Historically, the North East has played a pivotal role in shaping Britain's story. Perhaps its most iconic landmark is Hadrian's Wall, constructed by the Romans in AD 122–8 as a northern frontier for their empire. Stretching from the River Tyne in the east to the Solway Firth in the west, the wall remains a symbol of the region's ancient past. Centuries later, the North East saw waves of Viking invasions, as Norsemen navigated its rivers and coastal inlets, leaving behind a legacy that can still be traced in place names and cultural traditions.

ABOVE The Northern Sup Race Team at Derwent Reservoir.

The region's geography is just as captivating as its history. The dramatic coastline features the Cleveland Way's rugged cliffs and Northumberland's sandy beaches and picturesque fishing villages like Craster and Seahouses. Inland, rolling hills and expansive moorlands dominate the landscape, with the North Pennines National Landscape and Northumberland National Park offering unspoiled wilderness for exploration. The mighty rivers of the Tyne, Tees and Wear wind their way through the countryside, providing opportunities for paddling through serene rural stretches or beneath the industrial architecture of the region's cities.

Durham City stands as a jewel of the region, with its stunning cathedral and castle, both UNESCO World Heritage Sites. The city blends historical grandeur with vibrant modern life, offering riverside paddling opportunities alongside a rich cultural scene.

Lakes and reservoirs offer tranquil settings for water-based activities, while the North Sea's bracing waters provide a challenge, with hidden coves and abundant wildlife, including seals and seabirds, making for unforgettable paddling experiences.

Whether you're exploring its waterways, delving into its rich history or enjoying its varied landscapes, the North East of England is a destination that truly has something for everyone. Its unique blend of the ancient and the contemporary, the natural and the man-made, ensures a memorable experience for all who visit.

BELOW View from Prebends Bridge showing Durham Cathedral and Castle on the right with the old Corn Mill opposite.

# 01

# BERWICK-UPON-TWEED

Berwick-upon-Tweed is England's northernmost town, sitting at the mouth of the 156km-long River Tweed, one of Britain's great salmon rivers. Uniquely, it's the only river in England that doesn't require a rod licence. With options to paddle up the river or head out to the ocean, Berwick has something for all paddlers.

## The Lowdown

**DIFFICULTY**

**WATER TYPE** Sea, estuary

**DISTANCE** Variable
**Paddle 1:** up to 15km (round trip)
**Paddle 2:** 5km (round trip)

**PARKING** Car park

**WHAT3WORDS** ///crash.spirit.jokes

**LAUNCH** Bankside

## A brief history

The border town of Berwick-upon-Tweed, situated at the mouth of the River Tweed, has had a turbulent history. Until 1482, when it was captured by the Duke of Gloucester (later Richard III), it had changed hands many times during the Anglo-Scottish wars.

There are rumours that today Berwick is at war with Russia. This is in fact not true: the legend stems from a historical quirk. The story goes that when the Treaty of Paris was signed in 1856, ending the Crimean War, Berwick-upon Tweed was mistakenly left out of the peace treaty. As the town had been mentioned in

BERWICK-UPON-TWEED

Finish   Start

UNION CHAIN
BRIDGE

declarations of war but not in the peace settlement, this oversight meant Berwick was still technically at war! The tale was further popularised when in 1966 a Soviet official was said to have visited Berwick and jokingly declared peace on behalf of Russia, ending the 110-year conflict. There are no official records of this, and it remains a charming piece of local folklore, highlighting the town's unique historical and geopolitical position.

## The paddle
This launch spot offers two different paddles, both of which are best attempted either side of high tide. It helps ensure easy access to the water and slower, calmer waters.

BELOW A train running over the Royal Border Bridge.

### Paddle 1: Berwick to Union Chain Bridge (up to 15km)
From the parking area, follow the path and access the water upstream from the Royal Border Bridge. Heading west, keeping to the nearside bank takes you into Yarrow Slake, a large, mostly enclosed pool that is full at high tide but drains as the tide goes out. This is great to gain confidence or just have a good mess about before rounding the corner and heading up the river. Either side of high tide the river is slow-moving, allowing for an easy and relaxed paddle. After 2.5km you reach the A1 road bridge and the point where the tidal effect starts to ease. You can either turn round or continue as the river winds its way, passing woodlands and open fields and eventually reaching the Union Chain Bridge, a suspension bridge that marks the border with England and Scotland, at 7.5km.

### Paddle 2: Berwick to the sea (5km)
Launching from the same spot, if you paddle upstream before turning and heading through the bridge piers you are treated to a spectacular view of Berwick framed by three bridges that span the river. Line up and paddle through the centre of the arch to avoid any debris that may be hidden below the surface. On the right is Berwick Amateur Rowing Club, whose members regularly train on the river when tides and weather

allow. Pass under the Royal Tweed Bridge, opened in 1928 to help ease traffic over the Berwick Bridge, commonly known as the Old Bridge, just 100m further down. Once past the Old Bridge, the river opens out with the industrial port to the right and the old town to the left. The main river curves around the south bank; at lower tides, the north side can be quite shallow and the beach of Sandstell Point opposite the pier grows and shrinks with the ebb and flow of the tide. At the end of the pier is the red and white lighthouse, one of the stops on the Lowry Trail. If you have lost track of time and spent longer than intended here, the flow of the water as you return up the river can be quite strong, particularly through the arches at the Old Bridge, so aim for the centre and you will soon be past. For this route, I would recommend trying to keep close to high tide if you are a newer paddler.

## Wildlife

The Tweed Estuary has become famous for its immense colony of **mute swans** – it's the second largest in Britain. On occasions, almost 800 swans have been counted on the river.

## Food stops

• **The Lookout café** in Berwick is a hidden gem tucked under the Old Bridge, offering light lunches and snacks.
• **Marshalls Cafe** in Scremerston is a family-run café offering breakfast, brunch and incredible cake and sweet treats.

## Getting there

• **By car** – Berwick is situated just off the A1.
• **By train** – Berwick is on the East Coast Main Line. The station is at the opposite end of the rail bridge to the paddle launch site.
• **By bus** – The nearest bus stop is Pudding Lane, a 10-minute walk away.

## Other activities

• **The Lowry Trail** L.S. Lowry was a frequent visitor to Berwick. The trail is a self-guided trip around the town, exploring the sites where he produced many of his most important paintings and sketches.
• **Berwick Barracks and Main Guard** Following the Jacobite rising in 1715, the town's defences were upgraded, and the Barracks and Main Guard were built. Today, it's one of the town's biggest tourist attractions.

## NEED TO KNOW

■ There are no toilets available at the launch site.

■ No licence is needed to paddle the River Tweed.

■ This section of the River Tweed is tidal so always check tide times before heading out. There is enough water to paddle even at low tide; however, low tide involves a short walk over kelp, which is often rather slippery.

## ANECDOTE FROM BERWICK-UPON-TWEED

*A few years ago, I worked for Northern Bootcamp, a fantastic health and fitness retreat that encourages residents and guests to try a wide range of outdoor activities. They could experience everything from archery and hammer-throwing to bushcraft skills, shelter building, hiking and rock climbing. Maybe not surprisingly, my favourite activities were the paddle sports. We would load up the big trailer with open Canadian canoes and kayaks and head up to Berwick for an afternoon of paddle fun on the river.*

*Maybe it's now time for me to make a little confession: our canoes were two-seaters and sometimes I would pair up and sit in the rear seat. There was nothing unusual about that, but on one particular occasion – and I will not name any names for my own protection – we were all making our way down to the mouth of the river, where there is a nice sandbank, perfect for a spot of lunch. There was a little bit of a breeze on our faces, nothing of any significance at all, but I decided to have a little bit of fun. I hate to admit it, but as I delivered my most enthusiastic motivational speech, I urged my paddling partner to paddle harder into the 'wind' – otherwise, I warned, we risked being left behind by the others. While they 'dug deep' and gave it their all, I was sitting back, paddle out of the water, munching on an extra protein snack I'd sneaked into my pocket before setting off! I would like to say this was a one-off, but sadly, it became a tactic I used on more than one occasion!*

LEFT The remains of an old fishing pontoon.

BELOW A swan taking off at the mouth of the River Tweed.

# 02 FARNE ISLANDS

Located 3–8km off the coast of Bamburgh, the rugged Farne Islands form an archipelago of 15 to 28 islands, their number shifting with the tides. Designated as a National Nature Reserve and Site of Special Scientific Interest, Inner Farne is an ideal place to see some spectacular wildlife.

## The Lowdown

**DIFFICULTY** 🌢🌢🌢++

**WATER TYPE** Sea

**DISTANCE** 8km (round trip)

**PARKING** Car park

**WHAT3WORDS** ///twinkling.atom.arrival

**LAUNCH** Beach

RIGHT Stopping to take in the views of the castle after a paddle around Inner Farne.

## A brief history

The Farne Islands are steeped in history. After serving as prior of Lindisfarne Monastery on the nearby Holy Island for 12 years, St Cuthbert retired to the solitude of Inner Farne in AD 676. While living there, he introduced laws to protect the eider ducks and other seabirds that nested on the island. These laws are believed to be the earliest bird protection measures in the world.

The islands are perhaps most famous for the story of Grace Darling. On 7 September 1838, a paddle steamer named the *Forfarshire* became shipwrecked on Harcar Rock. Grace's father, William, was

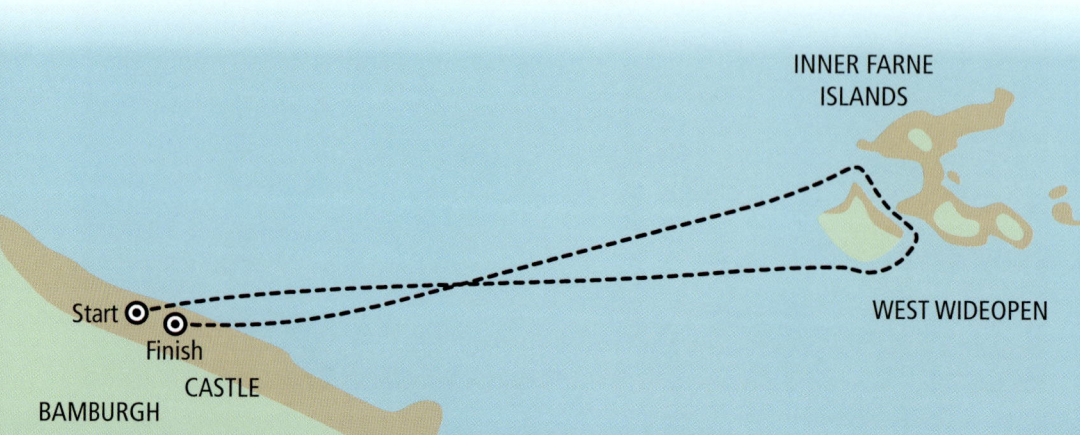

INNER FARNE ISLANDS

WEST WIDEOPEN

Start

Finish

CASTLE

BAMBURGH

the lighthouse keeper on Longstone. Grace, who was just 22 years old at the time, set off with her father in their rowing boat and rescued the nine survivors in gale-force winds and thick fog.

## The paddle

For me, the best place to set off on this epic paddle is the beach below the magnificent Bamburgh Castle – a true jewel in the crown of northern England. A height barrier of 2.05m has been fitted to the car park entrance. You can also park in the main village car park (///bead.majors.schooling), cross the road, and follow the path through the dunes to the east of the castle. It's an approximately 550m walk.

Before launching, make sure you have obtained a stamped permit from the National Trust trailer at Seahouses harbour.

Then take a moment to to appreciate the stunning views. Behind you stands the breathtaking Bamburgh Castle, while to the north, Bamburgh Lighthouse marks the coastline. Beyond that, you can see the Holy Island of Lindisfarne. Looking east out to sea, the Farne Islands stretch across the horizon. Our destination is Inner Farne, easily recognisable – not just because it's the closest island to shore – but because, to me, there appears to be an aeroplane taking off! In reality, it's just the roof of the building next to the lighthouse.

Launching from the beach and heading straight for Inner Farne, it's a 3.5km crossing. The sea state can shift from silky smooth to slightly more challenging as you pass over rocks deep below the surface. The Farne Islands are formed from an outcrop of Whin Sill, the hard igneous rock that supports Bamburgh Castle. Depending on the time of year, you may be deafened by a cacophony of noise from the vast number of nesting seabirds, or find yourself surrounded by inquisitive seals swimming out to investigate as you paddle by.

Paddling round the south side of the island offers stunning views of the birds nesting in the cliffs before rounding to the north. Here, you pass through a narrow channel between Inner Farne and West Wideopen Island, known as 'Wideopen Gut'. The current can rush through this section creating some disturbed waters, so it's best to keep to the left-hand side closest to shore. Keep an eye out for a jetty and small beach about halfway along. Landing on Inner Farne is permitted from April to September. If you prefer to stay on the water, then just past the jetty lies a sheltered area called 'The Kettle' – a perfect stop to rest and have a snack, while taking in the beautiful surroundings.

When you're ready to leave, continue following the island's coastline until Bamburgh Castle comes into view. Heading towards the castle, you'll be treated to a unique perspective that few people ever get to experience. From there, it's just a short paddle along the coast back to your starting point.

## Wildlife
Sir David Attenborough once described the Farne Islands as his 'favourite place in the UK to take in nature at its best'. In the summer, the islands turn into an aviation wonderland. Expect to see a host of seabirds including puffins; eider ducks; cormorants; shags; fulmars; kittiwakes; arctic; common and sandwich terns, guillemots and razorbills.

The Farne Islands are home to one of the largest populations of Atlantic grey seals – at times, the numbers can reach 4,000. While paddling over to Inner Farne, you may also encounter harbour porpoises and bottlenose dolphins. Minke whales and basking sharks have been known to visit this area too.

## Food stops
• The Potted Lobster in Bamburgh serves a menu brimming with fresh, locally sourced ingredients. Their dishes celebrate the flavours of the Northumberland coast, offering guests an authentic taste of the region's best seafood in a really cosy and inviting setting.
• The Copper Kettle Tearoom in Bamburgh is a traditional tearoom serving homemade light-bite snacks and sweet treats.
• If you're craving fish and chips, head over to Seahouses, where you'll find several excellent options. My favourite is Lewis's Fish Restaurant, which offers both dine-in and takeaway options.

## Getting there
• By car – Follow the B1341 into Bamburgh village. At the Y-junction, go across into The Wynding. Follow this road for about 500m and the car park is on your right.
• By train – The most convenient stations to Bamburgh are Berwick and Alnmouth, on the East Coast Main Line.
• By bus – The Arriva X18 bus runs between Berwick and Alnwick, stopping at Bamburgh, opposite The Lord Crewe hotel.

## Other activities
• If you would like to explore the outer islands, boat trips sail from Seahouses all year round. For more information, see www.farne-islands.com.
• A castle has been standing guard above Bamburgh village for over 1,400 years.

RIGHT Getting ready to launch from Bamburgh Beach with the Farne Islands in the distance.

Immerse yourself in the present castle's rich history and admire the coastal views from the battlements.

• The Holy Island of **Lindisfarne** is another must-visit location. Drive along the 5km causeway or, if you're feeling adventurous, follow the waymarked posts and walk across the tidal sands of the Pilgrim's Way. This historic pass has been used by saints, monks, bishops and pilgrims since the 7th century.

• **Bamburgh Castle Golf Club** lies at the far end of The Wynding, a stunning links course with glorious views of the Northumberland coastline.

BELOW Inner Farne lighthouse.

## NEED TO KNOW

■ This can be a very challenging paddle and should only be attempted on a calm day with flat sea. It's also best on a neap tide either side of high tide – a good website for tide information is www.tideschart.com. Windy.app and swellmap.com are good sites for checking the sea state.

■ Never attempt this paddle with offshore winds.

■ There are no toilets in the car park, but there are public toilets in the village.

■ The seal breeding season is October to December, so it is best to avoid paddling to the Farnes around this time.

■ You must obtain a permit to paddle from the National Trust trailer at Seahouses harbour before you set off.

### ANECDOTE FROM THE FARNE ISLANDS

*I spent many childhood holidays on the beach at Bamburgh playing in the waves, making sandcastles, or just staring out at mystical islands, near yet so far away. Fascinated by tales of huge waves, storms and the incredible story of Grace Darling and her father's daring rescue of nine sailors from the wreck of the SS Forfarshire, I would sit in the dunes under the castle studying the movement of the water. I planned how I could make my way to the islands under my own power instead of using the pleasure boats that set sail from nearby Seahouses.*

*Fast-forward 30 years and it was time to turn that schoolboy dream into reality. Dan Smith – owner of Northern Outdoor and Northern Bootcamp – and I set ourselves a 12-hour endurance challenge to paddle out and circumnavigate the Farne Islands, the purpose being twofold: first, to raise money for a defibrillator for the local area, and second, to help Dan prepare for his upcoming 'Paddle of Britain'. (He became the first person to kayak from the most northerly part of Scotland through the inland waterways, finally ending at the English Channel.)*

*We had been waiting for a rare weather window of a neap tide combined with next to no wind. On 29 August 2019, the day arrived – not quite zero wind but good enough. The plan was to paddle out past Megstone on the far left, Dan was in his trusty kayak 'Tommy' and I was on my favourite Naish Maliko SUP. We would head to Inner Farne and then complete a full loop of the visible islands, heading around Longstone, then back down to Inner Farne, and repeat for 12 hours, exploring as much of the islands as we could along the way.*

*Heading out from shore, the conditions were almost perfect. Silky smooth waters helped us make quick progress around Megstone and it wasn't long before we arrived at Inner Farne. It was quite tempting to hang around and explore, but with the knowledge the wind was likely to pick up we decided to push on and complete our first lap. We had around 2.5km of open ocean before reaching the middle block of islands of Brownsman and Staple. We stopped for a quick drink, excited to get to Longstone and its famous lighthouse. As we made our way around the far side, there was a noticeable change in the sea state – a good indication that we made the right choice to do a full lap before exploring the nooks and crannies. Rounding Longstone, we had a fun but challenging 5km downwind run back to Inner Farne.*

*We stopped again for a brew and a bite to eat – you can land at Inner Farne for a small charge if you are a National Trust member. On our second lap, the conditions deteriorated quite rapidly. There were sections of glass water separated by areas with 5-foot standing waves. Over time, the calm spots gradually disappeared and after nine hours of paddling and exploring and finding sheltered spots, we made the decision to head back to the mainland. It took nearly an hour to get back to shore and we finished our last two hours of paddling from Seahouses to Budle Bay.*

*It was a fantastic day spent with a great mate, sharing our love for expeditions and exploration. To my knowledge, I am still the only person to circumnavigate the entire range of islands on a stand-up paddleboard. This is a challenge suitable only for the most experience paddlers. Taking all necessary safety precautions is essential. On a good day, paddling to Inner Farne can also be a great little adventure – again, with all safety measures in place.*

# 03 BEADNELL BAY

Beadnell Bay spans 3km of pristine golden sand, offering an unspoiled haven of natural beauty. Flanked by picturesque sand dunes, this crescent-shaped beach provides natural protection from the North Sea. This unique geography results in calm, sheltered waters, making it an ideal location for paddlesports and other water activities. Whether you're a seasoned paddler or relatively new to the water, Beadnell Bay offers something for everyone.

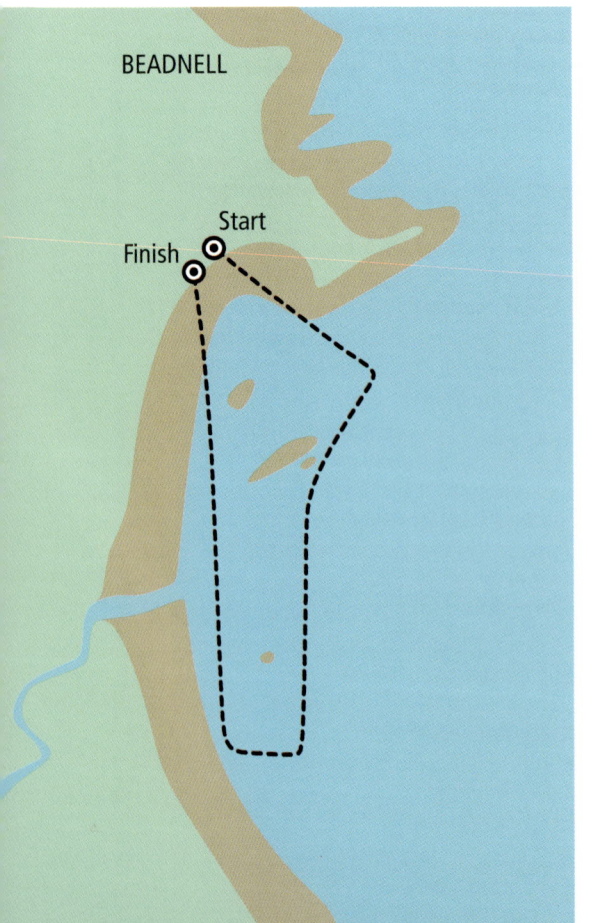

BEADNELL

Start
Finish

## The Lowdown

**DIFFICULTY** ⬤ to ⬤⬤⬤

**WATER TYPE** Sea

**DISTANCE** Up to 5km

**PARKING** Beadnell Bay car park

**WHAT3WORDS** ///welfare.raced.daredevil

**LAUNCH** Beach

BELOW A bank holiday at Beadnell Bay.

## A brief history

The village of Beadnell dates back to medieval times. A tower house – built as a lookout in the 16th century to protect the village from Scottish invaders – still stands proudly today as part of the Craster Arms village pub. Once a thriving fishing village, Beadnell's harbour was built in the 18th century, mainly to support the export of limestone from the local quarries. Over time, the lime kilns adjacent to the harbour were used by the local fishermen to cure their herring. Today, the kilns are owned by the National Trust and are open to the public.

## The paddle

From the car park, it's only a short walk through the dunes to the beach. A lot of work has been done over the last few years to help protect the dunes, so please only use the designated paths to avoid unnecessary erosion. The bay is a fantastic spot for paddlers of all abilities; at high tide, it fills up, creating a nice area for leisurely paddling and building confidence for those with little experience of sea paddling. Avoid entering the harbour – this is a small working harbour and, although not strictly banned, it's better to keep to the bay area. Paddling past the harbour wall, you are still protected from southerly swells by the rocks off Beadnell Point. If you head down the bay, you can just make out the ruins of Dunstanburgh Castle, one of many castles along the north-east coastline.

As the tide recedes, two large reefs swaying with kelp start to emerge in the centre of the bay. These create a deep channel, inviting you to navigate through. At the opposite end of the bay, nearer High Newton-by-the-Sea, the waves tend to gain more momentum and it's a popular spot for some SUP surfing. Notably, thanks to the bay's protection and the gentle sloping beach, the water inside the bay is surprisingly warm, a stark contrast to the cooler temperatures typically associated with the North Sea.

## Wildlife

The bay is a haven for both seabirds and marine life. White-beaked and bottlenose dolphins can regularly be seen swimming up the coastline. Grey seals bask on the rocks just past the harbour. Further round the bay, Long Nanny Burn runs into the beach and is a protected nature reserve, home to a colony of little terns and the largest mainland colony of Arctic terns in the UK. Also keep an eye out for puffins and gannets while out on the water.

## Food stops

• The Landing in Beadnell Bay is a modern restaurant located 100m from the bay. It's open all day, serving hot and cold food and drinks.
• Beadnell Towers in Beadnell village

offers a more upmarket dining experience, with a focus on fresh, locally sourced ingredients and seasonal produce.

• **Craster Arms** in Beadnell village is a bustling traditional pub and restaurant serving quality food. There's plenty of outside and inside dining.

• **Saltwater Café Bar & Bistro** in Beadnell village offers quality light snacks, hearty meals, and teas and coffees.

# Getting there

• **By car** – Follow the B1340 into Beadnell. As you reach the seafront, turn right and follow the road around to the car park.

• **By train** – The nearest station is Alnmouth on the East Coast Main Line.

• **By bus** – Take the Arriva X18 from Alnwick via Alnmouth to Beadnell. The bus stop at Harbour Road is closest to the seafront.

## Other activities

• **KA Adventure Sports** are based in the car park. They rent out SUPs and sit-on-top kayaks as well as offering a range of watersport tuition from surfing and kitesurfing to stand-up paddleboarding. They also deliver coasteering trips in various locations along the nearby coastline.

• **The Northumberland Coast Path**, a long-distance 100km walk from Cresswell to Berwick, runs past the bay.

• The ruins of the 14th-century **Dunstanburgh Castle** lie 10km south of Beadnell.

• The North East is renowned for some special golf courses. **Seahouses** and **Bamburgh** are open to the public, offering stunning views of castles and coastline.

## NEED TO KNOW

■ Toilets are available in the car park.

■ There are no lifeguards on duty.

■ Dogs are allowed on the beach; however, during the nesting season restrictions are in place where dogs must be kept on leads.

■ Weaver fish are known to bury themselves in the sand, so if you are paddling at low tide it's best to wear water shoes.

LEFT TOP The bay at low tide.

LEFT BOTTOM Beadnell Harbour (credit Natalie Agars).

RIGHT TOP Taking my racing board to the sea.

RIGHT BOTTOM Team KA Dragon Board racing (credit Michael Fawcus).

# 04 LADYBURN LAKE – DRURIDGE BAY COUNTRY PARK

**Sitting in the heart of Druridge Bay Country Park,** which comprises woodlands, grasslands, beaches and sand dunes, lies Ladyburn Lake, a 25-acre, 4.5m-deep fresh-water lake that is just perfect for paddling. Encircled by a wheelchair-accessible trail, Ladyburn Lake is an ideal location for all the family.

## The Lowdown

**DIFFICULTY**

**WATER TYPE** Lake

**DISTANCE** Variable. 2km circumference

**PARKING** Druridge Bay Country Park watersports car park

**WHAT3WORDS** ///furniture.blaze.doted

**LAUNCH** Slipway

RIGHT TOP Ladyburn Lake.

RIGHT BOTTOM The view from the launch slipway.

Start

Finish

## A brief history

Ladyburn Lake began life in the early 1970s, created on the remains of the Coldrife surface coal mine and fed by the gently flowing Lady Burn. However, its beauty didn't last long with the water leaking out through old mine workings, and by 1974 the lake was completely dry. In 1983, work began to restore the lake using clay from the nearby coalfields to line the bottom, enabling it to hold water, and it was officially reopened in 1989 as part of Druridge Bay Country Park.

## The paddle

Day, week or annual permits for paddling can be purchased from the café and visitor centre by the main car park. When walking towards the building, see if you can spot the little bee and insect hotel hidden in the trees. Once you have your permit, access to the lake is from the

watersports car park to the south-east end of the lake. From the bankside you can see pretty much the whole of the lake, and the view from here is a good opportunity to assess the conditions. One of the advantages of paddling on Ladyburn Lake is that if the wind is blowing, there is always somewhere to find a sheltered section to paddle. It's not unusual to see a bevy of swans guarding the little slipway to the water but don't be alarmed, they are used to seeing people and are generally happy to sit and watch you walk by with your board or boat.

On the water you will see a number of buoys seemingly scattered at random, but actually they follow the circumference of the lake. If you paddle alongside them, you will complete a 1.6km loop. However, the whole of the lake is available for you to use and explore.

From the slipway, heading left to the far west end of the lake, you come to the Druridge Bay Stepping Stones. They provide a shortcut for the walking path that surrounds the lake and can be such a quiet, peaceful part of the water. I'll leave it to you to count the number of steps. Looking back gives some lovely views over the park and listening to the water trickle over the weir is so relaxing. Follow the lake round the north section, passing the woodlands until you reach the footbridge, where the water drains out and flows into the North Sea.

As you continue, the loop passes a jetty used by Coquet Shorebase Trust, a community-based charity. The trust utilises

RIGHT A sign pointing the way from the lake to the beach.

BELOW Stepping stones.

water-based activities to help those who feel disenfranchised to develop the self-confidence to become active members of the community. At the lake, they provide stand-up paddleboard, kayak and sailing lessons. More information can be found on their website, www.coquetshorebase.org.uk.

From here, continue following the shoreline to complete the loop. Fishing is not allowed on the lake so you can paddle close to the shore, safe in the knowledge you won't be caught by any stray fishing hooks. However, do be mindful and respectful of the local wildlife that has made its home in the reeds and bullrushes.

## Wildlife

With its location so close to the coast, it's a haven for birdlife. Bullfinches, crossbills and redpolls are regular visitors, as well as the resident swans.

## Food stops

• Inside the visitor centre is a café selling hot and cold meals and a wide selection of teas and coffees (a favourite of mine is their millionaire's shortbread). There is also an abundance of benches and tables around the park if you want to bring your own picnic.
• The park is 4.8km south of the fishing town of Amble, home to the exquisite seafood restaurant The Old Boat House, situated on the waterfront.

## Getting there

• By car – Druridge Bay Country Park lies just off the A1068, 4.8km south of Amble and 9.6km east of the main A1 trunk road.
• By train – The nearest train stations are Widdrington and Morpeth.
• By bus – The nearby village of Hadston can be reached by MAX X20 bus from Newcastle and Alnwick or the MAX X18 bus from Morpeth.

## Other activities

• As well as the circular walking trail around the lake, the park has many paths winding through the woodlands and meadows.
• The sandy beach adjacent to the park stretches 5km.
• Swimming is allowed in the lake without a permit, but it is advised to wear a swim buoy.
• Adjacent to the visitor centre there is a well-maintained children's play park and large playing field.

## NEED TO KNOW

■ A permit (obtained from the visitor centre) is required before paddling.

■ There are several toilets inside the visitor centre.

■ There's a changing area inside the visitor centre.

# 05 HEXHAM TYNE GREEN

**The River Tyne is widely regarded as the best salmon fishing river in England.** Hexham Tyne Green is a beautiful and well-maintained country park situated after the confluence of the South Tyne and North Tyne at Warden Rock. Overlooked by the 19th-century stone road bridge, with an easy get-in and calm water, it's a perfect spot for beginners to gain confidence or those wishing to build fitness to join Northern SUP Race Club for Friday night intervals.

## The Lowdown

**DIFFICULTY**

**WATER TYPE** River

**DISTANCE** 2km+

**PARKING** Tyne Green Country Park car park

**WHAT3WORDS** ///winded.release.pave

**LAUNCH** Jetty

### A brief history
Opened in 1887 to commemorate Queen Victoria's Golden Jubilee, Tyne Green was gifted by Lord Allendale as a pleasure ground for local people. It was designated a country park in 1982, and has expanded to over 19ha, including open green spaces, a café, a golf course, children's play areas and walking routes aplenty. Tyne Green is the gateway to the historic 7th-century market town of Hexham and has become a popular destination for outdoor enthusiasts and watersports.

Turn before piers

Start

Finish

## The paddle

Access to the water is via the landing jetty near the bridge. There is plenty of free parking along the length of the park, but it's worth parking near the entrance, leaving only a short walk across the green to the launch spot. Once on the water, head in a westerly direction away from the bridge and weir. It's a flat 800m paddle upstream before the river splits at the island. From here, you can choose to stay in the lower section of the river, which is perfect for a bit of fitness training, skill development or just playing around. Alternatively, continue on past the island. The left-hand channel is approximately 100m of fast-flowing water and best avoided for SUP paddlers due to the flow and underwater entrapment hazards; Hexham Canoe Club use this section for whitewater slalom training. To the right side of the island, the water level can get quite shallow, so care is needed, and, depending on water levels,

ABOVE Another training session completed.

you may need to get off the board and walk a few metres until the water deepens again. Once past the island, there is another 800m stretch towards the remains of the old railway bridge stanchions. This section of the river is secluded and almost always deserted, providing the perfect opportunity to pitch up at one of the sandy beaches and watch the local wildlife.

On the first weekend in November, the River Tyne plays host to one of Europe's largest mass participation paddle events. Organised by Hexham Canoe Club, the Tyne Tour covers an 11km stretch of the river, starting in the village of Barrasford, through Warden Gorge, and finishing at the steps of the Green.

## Wildlife

Hexham is a popular spot for fishing, with dace, chub and brown trout the most popular. It is also common to see salmon and sea trout jumping and making their way to spawning grounds further up the river. Otters have been seen playing in the river, so keep an eye out past the island. Oystercatchers, purple sandpipers and herons are just some of the many species of birdlife that inhabit this section of river.

## Food stops

Off the water, there are several picnic benches and open spaces to enjoy a picnic, or towards the west end of the park, near the golf course, is Café Enna, offering hot and cold home-cooked meals, snacks and coffee. Hexham town centre is a 5-minute drive away and offers many coffee shops, pubs and restaurants.

## Getting there

• By car – Located on the south bank of the River Tyne, just off the A69 towards the town of Hexham.
• By train – Hexham train station is a 5-minute walk away.
• By bus – X84, X85 buses from Newcastle to Hexham bus station.

## Other activities

• Within the park, there is plenty to do when off the water. The play park is not only for children – adults can also join in and take on the little obstacle course. The golf club is open to non-members, and you can hire clubs with prior arrangement.
• Housesteads Roman Fort is approximately 20km north-west of Hexham. It is the most complete example of a Roman fort in Britain and well worth a tour. The fort stands proudly on Hadrian's Wall, which runs 117km from Bowness-on-Solway in the west to Wallsend in the east.

LEFT The launch jetty on the river.

BELOW George enjoying a cool off.

ABOVE Canoes lined up at the side of the river (credit Karen Greener).

BELOW The sun rising over Hexham Bridge.

# NEED TO KNOW

■ Hexham Rowing Club is based here so if they are training on the water, let the coach know you are there. They may ask you to keep more to one side of the river.

■ The river flow is mostly very gentle; however, with heavy rain the levels can change quite quickly so always check weather forecasts. The government flood website (check-for-flooding.service.gov.uk) and river webcam (www.farsondigitalwatercams.com/ locations/hexham) are excellent resources.

■ Well-behaved dogs are welcome in both the park and the water, so keep an eye out for swimming dogs as well as swimming humans.

■ Toilets are available.

■ There are no specific changing facilities in the park.

## ANECDOTE FROM HEXHAM TYNE GREEN

*Hexham Tyne Green may not be the longest stretch of water for paddling, but it's where Northern SUP Race Team – and my love for SUP – truly began. Back in 2017, a small group of us started meeting on Thursday afternoons to train, fall in, and have a laugh with each other. Then afterwards, we'd head to the local café to refuel and swap ideas on how we could improve, as well as sharing stories of our past adventures. We became great friends and, looking back now, it was a really special time.*

*As we continued to paddle through the autumn and the temperatures started to drop, talk began to turn to the winter, and how we could stay motivated to keep paddling through the colder months. I had recently competed as a novice in my first SUP race at the National Club Championships, hosted by Bray Lake Watersports in Berkshire. The whole experience was incredible. I've always loved sports and used to run and compete in triathlons, but I can honestly say that nothing I had done before could have prepared me for the unique experience of a SUP event. The community was so supportive and encouraging.*

*Driving home that night, I just knew I wanted to compete in every race the following year. Forming a race club was the logical step to help me to continue paddling throughout a cold northern winter. Northern SUP Race Team was born.*

*Today, we still meet regularly on the river for training and social paddles. If you ever see me out there on the river or sitting on a park bench enjoying a post-paddle picnic, please come over and say hello. I've always got time for a chat and to share a passion for SUP.*

BELOW George and Bruce with Hexham Bridge behind.

# 06 DERWENT RESERVOIR

Situated on the River Derwent, crossing the border of County Durham and Northumberland, and nestled in the North Pennines National Landscape, the 5.6km-long Derwent Reservoir is one of the largest inland waters in England. It's also home to Derwent Reservoir Sailing Club. With easy access to the water from well-maintained slipways, the calm water and stunning panoramic views provide the perfect location to enjoy a paddle on a sunny day.

## The Lowdown

**DIFFICULTY** 💧💧

**WATER TYPE** Lake

**DISTANCE** Variable – up to 9km circumference

**PARKING** Derwent Reservoir Sailing Club car park

**WHAT3WORDS** ///fruitcake.beaker.thumb

**LAUNCH** Slipway inside Derwent Reservoir Sailing Club

SAILING CLUB

Finish  Start

RESTRICTED AREA

RUFFSIDE

## A brief history

Construction of the Derwent Reservoir began in 1960; it was opened in July 1967 by Princess Alexandra to serve the houses and businesses of South Tyneside, Durham and Sunderland. Unlike other reservoirs in northern England, which are flooded valleys with a dam head, Derwent Reservoir was actually dug out of the ground, with the earth removed and then used to create the dam head. As the reservoir was filling up in 1966, a group of keen sailors approached the Sunderland & South Shields Water Company with a request to form a sailing club. Derwent Reservoir Sailing Club was established as a volunteer-led club and has been a resident of the reservoir since the opening day. In low-water years, remains can be seen of the three farms and two cottages demolished to allow construction of the reservoir, and occasionally an old road bridge is exposed.

As well as watersports, the area surrounding the reservoir has become a go-to for cyclists, with British Cycling annually hosting its National Road Series event 'Tour of the Reservoir' cycle race.

## The paddle

Derwent Reservoir Sailing Club is situated on the northside bank. Once you drive down the road to the barrier, press the buzzer and you will be let into the parking area. From here, it's a short walk to the sailing club building, where a club member will show you around the facilities and answer any questions.

Access to the water is from any one of the five gently sloping slipways. The area directly in front of the clubhouse is perfect for beginners to hone their skills before venturing further out to explore the stunning 3,500 acres of water available. Out on the water, paddlers can be assured of their safety with several rescue boats cruising up and down, ensuring paddlers and sailors have the best experience possible.

RIGHT Tobias and Bruce enjoying a training session (credit Jonah Schroeder).

BELOW An aerial view of Derwent Reservoir (credit Jonah Schroeder).

Nearly all the water is available to paddle except for the nature reserve to the far west of the reservoir. It's always worth heading up close and trying to spot some of the resident wildlife, including roe deer and ospreys. Paddling down eastwards towards the dam, stop off in Anchorage. It gained its name many years ago when sailors used to anchor their boats in the shallow water. Take a loop around the bay before continuing your journey, free to explore to your heart's content. For those more experienced, or who like longer paddles, a full trip around the circumference is approximately 9km, depending on water levels, so there are plenty of opportunities to paddle, chill and have fun in a clean and safe environment. Once you're finished paddling, head for a warm shower and then go for a bite to eat in the upstairs café. You can take in the views of the whole reservoir.

## Wildlife

There is plenty of wildlife to look out for while out on the water. Red kites, ospreys, barn owls and great crested grebes are among the birdlife that has made Derwent its home. Pow Hill Country Park, on the south side of the water, is home to a large population of red squirrels.

## Food stops

Once off the water, head upstairs to the Galley kitchen, which has a wide selection of hot and cold meals, snacks and drinks, as well as a licensed bar. Sitting on the balcony overlooking the water, watching the sailing boats and other paddlers, is a perfect way to finish off the day.

## Getting there

Due to its remote location 14.5km south of Corbridge, with no nearby train stations or regular bus routes, Derwent Reservoir Sailing Club is best accessed by car. For satnav, use the postcode DH8 9PT.

## Other activities

• **The club is RYA-affiliated** and offers excellent beginners' lessons in sailing and windsurfing, as well as supervised open water swimming sessions during the summer months.
• **Pow Hill Country Park**, on the south shore, offers some stunning short woodland walks that link up with a path taking in the views along the dam towards the observation tower and waterside park, a perfect place for young creative minds to play and explore the adventure playground.

BELOW The reservoir at sunset.

## NEED TO KNOW

■ The club is open weekends and Wednesdays from March to December.

■ There is a fee to launch on the reservoir, but included in the cost is the use of club wetsuits, buoyancy aids, paddleboards and kayaks. Visits can be booked in advance via www.drsc.co.uk.

■ Well-behaved dogs are allowed on site. However, owners are asked not to take them near the shoreline.

■ Toilet, shower and changing facilities are available.

■ Overnight camping facilities are also available.

# 07 RIVER TYNE – NEWBURN TO WYLAM

Paddling the serene yet dynamic River Tyne offers a unique and unforgettable opportunity to experience Newcastle's spectacular riverscape from the water. The River Tyne stretches for 118km from the Scottish borders in the north to Alston Moor in the south. The final tidal 27km take you from Wylam village through the cities of Newcastle and Gateshead, before eventually flowing into the North Sea at Tynemouth.

## The Lowdown

**DIFFICULTY**

**WATER TYPE** River

**DISTANCE** 7km (round trip)

**PARKING** Tyne Riverside Country Park car park

**WHAT3WORDS** ///chips.option.class

**LAUNCH** Slipway

BELOW Celebrating after a little race on the River Tyne.

## A brief history

The River Tyne has been integral to the region's history for centuries. In the early 20th century, it was known locally as 'the Coaly' due to the amount of coal transported from the local coal mines. It was not only a major trading route but also one of the world's leading shipbuilding centres. In recent years, the river has inspired many artists and musicians, including Dire Straits, Sting and Jimmy Nail. The seahorses on Newcastle United Football Club's badge symbolise the deep connection the Tyne has with the heart of the city.

## The paddle

Parking in Tyne Riverside Country Park car park, it's just a short walk to the access slipway to the water. The slipway is recessed slightly from the main river so as you head out and turn right, just

RIVERSIDE COUNTRY PARK

Start   Finish

check there is no traffic heading up the river from your left. This section of the Tyne is usually quiet; however, there are a couple of rowing clubs that use the river so take care and remember to always keep to the right-hand side. Once on the water, head west towards Wylam. The first kilometre, alongside Ryton Willows nature reserve, is quite wide and open, but once you pass the house on the south bank the river narrows slightly, and trees line both banks. It's easy to forget you are only a few miles outside of one of Britain's liveliest cities. The river winds its way peacefully through the countryside, with only the sounds of the birds, salmon jumping, or the occasional two-carriage train passing by to interrupt the silence.

Rounding the final curve, 3.5km from the start, you can see the Wylam Bridge crossing the river. There are rocks and small rapids before the bridge. This marks the end of the tidal section of the River Tyne and the turn-around point of the paddle. On the north bank, hidden behind the trees, is a little white cottage, the birthplace of the rail pioneer George Stephenson. Once you have turned round, if you have timed it well, it's

ABOVE Evening paddle heading towards Wylam.

BELOW Rowers training.

an easy paddle back downstream to the car park.

With this section of the River Tyne being tidal, I would recommend heading out

approximately one hour before high tide. If the tide is low, it is not always possible to reach as far as Wylam.

## Wildlife

With the River Tyne being one of the best salmon rivers in England, it's common to see them jumping clean out of the water, particularly in late summer and autumn. Grey seals are regularly seen as far up as Wylam and are always curious to investigate paddlers on the water. There have been reports of a turtle seen near the banks – rumour has it that it was released into the river some years ago and has survived, making the River Tyne its home.

## Food stops

• Elsie's Riverside Coffee Shop, located next to the car park, is dog friendly, sells home-cooked food, scones, cakes, sandwiches, teas, coffees, and the most amazing ice cream.
• The Keelman, Grange Road, Newburn, is a modern rural inn serving hot and cold meals and award-winning ales.

## Getting there

• By car – Tyne Riverside Park is situated 5km west of the A1, near Newcastle.

### NEED TO KNOW

■ Toilets are available in the café during opening hours.
■ A waterways licence is needed to paddle on the River Tyne.
■ This section of the River Tyne is tidal, so check tide times before paddling. I would avoid low tides as the access slipway can become quite slippery.

• By train – The nearest train station is Blaydon, situated on the Northern Rail Line between Newcastle and Carlisle.
• By bus – The nearest bus stop is Newburn High Street.

## Other activities

Tyne Riverside Country Park runs parallel to the river and covers 200 acres. There are children's play areas, an outdoor gym and numerous walking and cycling paths, including a riverside footpath to Wylam. This is part of the 135km Hadrian's Wall Path, which stretches from Wallsend to Bowness.

BELOW The glassy water at Newburn.

# 08 WHITLEY BAY – ST MARY'S LIGHTHOUSE

With over 2.5km of golden sands stretching from St Mary's Island to Whitley Bay, this is a very popular and easily accessible stretch of the north-east coastline. With the sheltered bay of Cullercoats next door, this area is the perfect place for all paddlesports.

## The Lowdown

| | |
|---|---|
| DIFFICULTY | ●●● |
| WATER TYPE | Sea |
| DISTANCE | 5km (round trip) |
| PARKING | Car park |
| WHAT3WORDS | ///flying.truly.grants |
| LAUNCH | Beach |

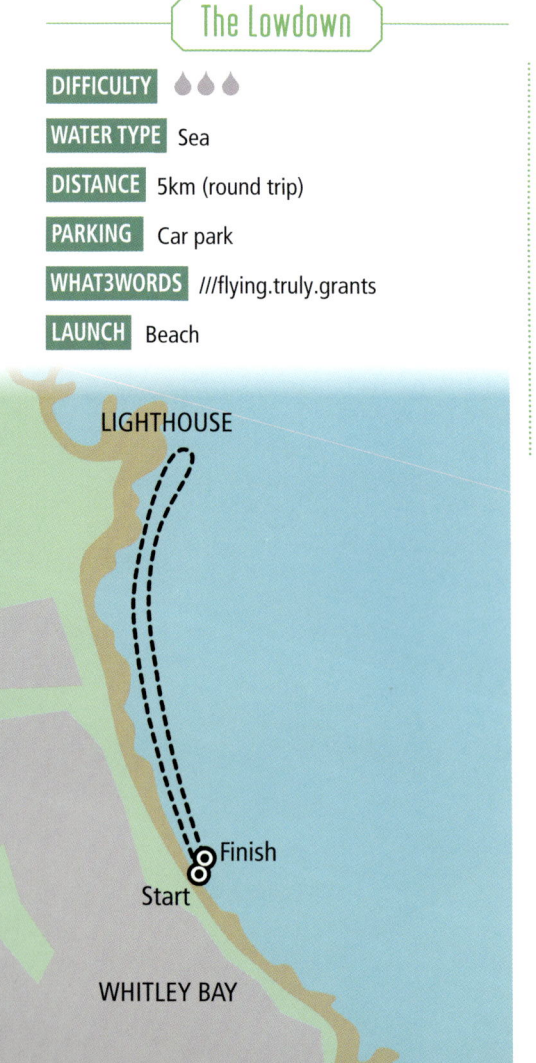

LIGHTHOUSE

Finish
Start

WHITLEY BAY

## A brief history

Whitley Bay became a popular seaside resort in the late 19th century, boosted by the North Tyneside Loop railway line reaching the town in 1882. This was much needed and helped counteract the declining local coal mining industry.

In 1896, work commenced to build a lighthouse on the small, rocky St Mary's Island. It was decommissioned in 1984 and is now a tourist attraction. If you climb the 137 steps to the top, you are rewarded with some spectacular views of the north-east coastline.

The Spanish City officially opened in 1908, its distinctive dome added two years later. Originally built as a concert hall and restaurant, it went on to become an iconic fairground, celebrated for its grand dome and striking architecture. Today, the building remains an important part of the town, housing many modern shops, bars, cafés and restaurants.

The picturesque harbour of Cullercoats lies 3km south of Whitley Bay. Once a small fishing village, it became a haven for artists in the 19th century. The American painter Winslow Homer spent time here, painting the local scenery and landscapes.

## The paddle

**Paddle 1: Spanish City to St Mary's Lighthouse** Launching from the sandy beach by the Spanish City, paddle north along the shoreline. In the distance, St Mary's Lighthouse stands prominently on its small island. At high tide, the island is isolated from the mainland, but as the tide recedes, a short causeway emerges, connecting it to the shore.

As you approach the far end of the beach, the sea state can start to change as the sea rebounds off the rocks and the sea wall that runs around the headland.

Another kilometre takes you up close to the lighthouse. After a quick selfie, it's time to turn around and head back.

In the distance, you can make out the ruins of Tynemouth Priory and Castle. Just to the right is the large white dome of the Spanish City, the start and finish point of the paddle. If you head in a straight line, it is easy to find yourself quite far from the shore, so always be mindful of your abilities and the conditions on the water. As you paddle further up, the priory disappears from view, but the Spanish City is unmissable and guides you back to the finish point.

**Paddle 2: Whitley Bay – Cullercoats Bay** Launching from the same location but heading south will take you to the quaint little bay of Cullercoats. This can be a more challenging paddle as there are no real options to get out until you reach the sheltered harbour of Cullercoats. This paddle follows the short, rocky cliffs, passing Brown's Bay and Point. Rocky outcrops are popular spots for anglers high up, who can be difficult to spot. On anything but the calmest days, the sea can

BELOW Cullercoats Bay (credit Karen Greener).

get choppy while passing the headland, but once past here the chop usually dies down and you have a more leisurely paddle into the beach. On the return paddle, you see St Mary's Lighthouse in the distance. Once again, don't be tempted to head straight for it, otherwise you can end up far from shore. At low tide, quite a few rocks and kelp beds become visible. These do help break up any rebounding swells, but don't get too close to avoid hitting your fin. Once around the headland, you will clearly see the dome of the Spanish City. You can now head straight for it to finish this epic paddle.

## Wildlife

Between spring and autumn, **bottlenose dolphins** are regular visitors to this coastline and are not afraid to come close and play around paddlers. The best chance to catch them is in the early morning or late afternoon.

Grey seals can be seen basking on the rocks at the foot of St Mary's Lighthouse.

## Food stops

• Whitley Bay has a host of **bars**, **restaurants** and **takeaways**. A favourite of mine is **Trenchers**, an upscale fish and chip shop, under the Spanish City dome.
• The lido has an ice cream and coffee kiosk, **Di Meo's**, located right on the seafront with picnic tables outside.

ABOVE Heading into Cullercoats with St George's Church in the background.

RIGHT Sunrise at St Mary's Lighthouse (credit Paul Carr).

BOTTOM RIGHT Paul enjoying a sunrise paddle into the caves near Cullercoats (his playground for over 50 years).

## Getting there

• **By car** – From the A19, take the A1058 signed Whitley Bay. At the second roundabout, the A193 to Whitley Bay brings you to the seafront. Bear left and follow to the car park.
• **By train** – The nearest station is Newcastle Central. From here, take the Tyne and Wear Metro Yellow Line to Whitley Bay.
• **By bus** – Arriva Bus 51 runs from Newcastle and stops in Whitley Bay, with only a short walk to the beach.

## Other activities

• **Northerly Swell Surfside Emporium** is located on Watts Slope and offers SUP lessons and rentals, including surfboards, kayaks and bikes.
• **The ruins of Tynemouth Priory and Castle** stand on a headland overlooking Tynemouth. A highlight is the little Percy Chantry Chapel, which survives intact in the priory church.

# NEED TO KNOW

■ Toilets are available on Watts Slope, situated just next to the beach launch spot.

■ Always check weather and tides before going on the water.

# 09 SUNDERLAND – ROKER TO SEABURN

The famous Sunderland 'Roker Roar' may have found a new home on the other side of the city, but Roker still has plenty to cheer about. Whether you're new to paddle sports or an experienced paddle surfer, the Blue Flag status of Roker beach and the golden sands of Seaburn are great locations to enjoy the ocean, relax, sunbathe or explore the shoreline, hunting for sea glass.

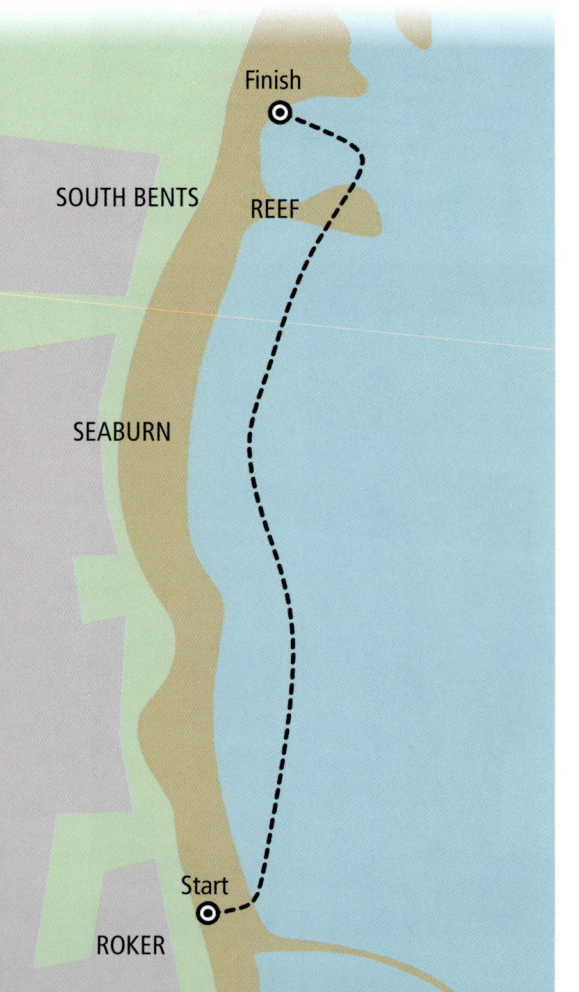

## The Lowdown

**DIFFICULTY**  ●● to ●●● depending on conditions

**WATER TYPE**  Sea

**DISTANCE**  5km (round trip)

**PARKING**  Harbour View car park

**WHAT3WORDS**  ///tips.basic.cloth

**LAUNCH**  Beach

## A brief history

The beaches of Roker and Seaburn were once separated by a magnesian limestone cliff known as Holy Rock. It got its name not from any religious connotations, but from holes and caves carved out in the rock by the ocean waves. By the 1930s, the soft, crumbling rock had become too unstable, and it was decided to demolish the front part of the rock and build the walkway joining the booming Roker resort to the Edwardian resort of Seaburn.

Seaburn was a favourite place of artist L.S. Lowry. One of his Seaburn seascape paintings was sold at auction for over a million pounds!

## The paddle

From Harbour View car park, it's only a short walk to Roker Harbour beach, which is a perfect spot for those new to paddling on the sea. Access to the water is from the soft, gently sloping sandy beach. The harbour piers offer plenty of protection from northerly and southerly sea swells, while still having the feel of being on the ocean. On the south side of the beach, the River Wear flows into the sea, passing between the piers. The river leads to Sunderland harbour and marina, so be mindful of boat traffic passing through. There is still plenty to explore while keeping clear of the river's path.

**Roker Beach to Seaburn** If you are looking to explore a little further, just to the left of the north pier wall is Roker beach, another beautiful sandy beach. From here, you paddle heading north towards Seaburn. Ahead you can see Meik's Lighthouse, known locally as the White Lighthouse; it's made of cast iron and was built in 1856 by Thomas Meik. The lighthouse was originally situated on Roker's Old South Pier but was

ABOVE Roker Pier from above.

relocated to Roker Cliff Park in the early 1980s. As you approach the lighthouse, you will see the Cat and Dog Steps leading up from the beach. There is a rather gruesome tale of how they got their name, but I'll leave that story out of a family book! Soon, you'll arrive at the sandy Seaburn beach.

## Wildlife

Porpoises and seals can be seen near to shore and have been known to swim quite close to paddlers.

In autumn and winter, the sandy beaches and rock pools provide food for purple sandpipers and turnstones migrating south from Scandinavia.

## Food stops

- There are many eateries along the seafront. Sue's Café and Grannie Annie's on Marine Walk are favourites of mine.
- If you are a fan of Asian cuisine then check out House of Zen at Seaburn, with

stunning views overlooking the sea and amazing food.

## Getting there

• **By car** – From the city centre, follow the A183 signed Roker Park. Once you reach the coast, signs for Roker beach bring you to the car park.

• **By train** – Sunderland station is on the Durham Coast Line and a 2.4km walk from Roker beach.

• **By bus** – The 18 bus stops at Harbour View. The route follows the A183 and has several stops along the way to Seaburn.

## Other activities

• **Sunderland Aquatic Centre** has a 50m swimming pool and separate diving pool.

• **Penshaw Monument** is a memorial to the 1st Earl of Durham that looks like a Greek temple. It sits in a prominent position on a hill near the village of Penshaw and is worth the climb for the views.

• **Silksworth Sports Complex and Ski Slope** is an outdoor ski and snowboard slope, suitable for all ages and abilities.

BELOW Between two piers.

# NEED TO KNOW

■ Public toilets are available on the promenade.

■ Always check local weather forecasts for wind speed and direction as well as sea state and wave heights before you set out. Only head out if you're competent in the conditions. Also, check the water quality and avoid Roker beach after periods of heavy rainfall due to possible debris and wastewater discharges. Useful links are www.sas.org.uk/water-quality/sewage-pollution-alerts/ and environment.data.gov.uk/bwq

RIGHT Simon by Roker Pier Lighthouse.

# 10 DURHAM RIVER WEAR

**The River Wear is a jewel in the North East of England,** rising in the Pennines and flowing easterly through County Durham, finally emptying into the North Sea in the city of Sunderland. At 96km in length, it's one of the region's longest rivers. The River Wear winds majestically through the centre of the cathedral city of Durham. Its tranquil waters are home to many species of wildlife, including kingfishers, herons and wild salmon, making it a haven for nature enthusiasts and paddlers alike.

## The Lowdown

**DIFFICULTY** 💧

**WATER TYPE**  River

**DISTANCE**  5km (round trip)

**PARKING**  Parking area

**WHAT3WORDS**  ///strong.quit.upgrading

**LAUNCH**  Jetty

## A brief history
The city of Durham was founded in AD 995 by Anglo-Saxon monks who sought a place to safeguard the remains of St Cuthbert from the invading Vikings. The original church they built lasted a hundred years before Durham Cathedral was constructed in 1093, a masterpiece of Norman architecture housing the shrines of both St Cuthbert and the Venerable Bede. Adjacent to the cathedral, Durham Castle was built under the orders of William the Conqueror to house the first Prince-Bishop,

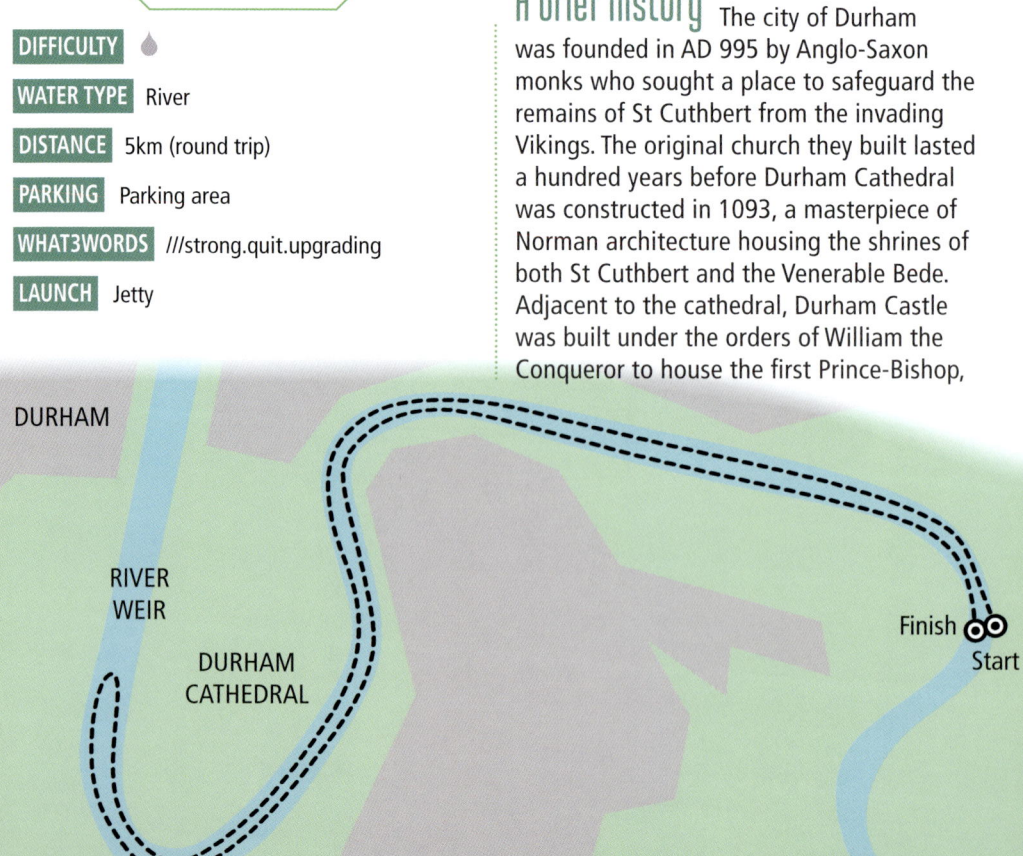

DURHAM

RIVER WEIR

DURHAM CATHEDRAL

Finish

Start

whose attempt to protect the kingdom from the unruly people of the north proved disastrous. His successor, Ranulf Flambard, one of the most notable bishops and known for his sharp wit, was the first person to be imprisoned in the Tower of London, after being arrested for financial mismanagement and extortion. He managed to escape by smuggling in a rope and getting his guards so drunk they fell asleep.

ABOVE Elvet Bridge.

## The paddle

From the car park, follow the slope leading down to the jetty and steps of the Durham Amateur Rowing Club. Heading left from the jetty takes you down towards the city. It's not long before you catch your first view of the majestic Durham Cathedral standing on the hill with its protector, Durham Castle, alongside. Both are inscribed on the World Heritage List because of their exceptional architectural innovation and history, along with their visual drama high up on the peninsula. Pass under a footbridge, then the New Elvert road bridge is quickly followed by the narrow stone arches of Elvet Bridge – built in the late 12th century, it is Durham's second-oldest bridge.

Soon, the river is banked on both sides by woodland, and you could easily be fooled into thinking you are deep in rural countryside, instead of the heart of a vibrant city. After another kilometre you come to Durham's most visited bridge, Prebends Bridge. Built in the 18th century, its location was chosen with the beauty of the landscape in mind. Once you pass the bridge, you can't miss the iconic Durham Cathedral up on the hill – it's a perfect opportunity for photos. Sit on the jetty for a snack and just admire the views. Although the water is slow-moving and easy to paddle against the flow, just be mindful and don't drift too close to the small weir before heading back up the river.

## Wildlife

The tranquil waters of the Wear are home to many species of wildlife including **kingfishers**, **herons** and **wild salmon** and, if you're lucky, you could spot the local **otters** playing in the banksides.

## Food stops

• Durham city centre has many fantastic eateries to choose from. Located next to the rowing club, **1860 Bar & Kitchen** is open every day 10am–2.30pm and serves hot and cold drinks, scones and sweet treats.
• **The Boat Club** is on the riverbank beside the Elvet Bridge with a cocktail bar on the ground floor and steakhouse upstairs. You can even paddle up to the Boat Club from the water.

## Getting there

• **By car** – From the A690, cross New Elvet Bridge. Turn left at the lights onto Old Elvet then left into Green Lane. As you approach the rowing club, there's an opening in a wooden fence on the left leading to a small gravel road. Follow this round to the parking area located next to the river.

• **By train** – The nearest train station is Durham on the East Coast Main Line, which runs from King's Cross to Edinburgh Waverley. It's 2.4km from the river.

• **By bus** – There is a good park-and-ride service in Durham that stops at Milburngate, 1.6km from the river.

## Other activities

• A visit to **Durham Cathedral** is a must. The huge vaulted ceilings are a sight to behold. Don't miss the famous Sanctuary Knocker on the North Door, a symbol of medieval justice. If you're feeling energetic, climb the stairs to the top of the tower for some majestic vistas over the city.

• The world-famous open-air **Beamish Museum**, around 14km north-west of Durham, takes you back in time to see what life was like in North East England in the 19th century and the first half of the 20th century. Tickets can be purchased from their website: www.beamish.org.uk.

RIGHT Michael, Tom and Simon by Durham Cathedral.

BELOW Michael by the old corn mill and Durham School Boathouse.

# NEED TO KNOW

■ Toilets are available at the rowing club.

■ The river is used by rowing clubs so aim to keep to the right-hand side.

## ANECDOTE FROM DURHAM CITY

*As a young boy, I spent many a Saturday taking the bus to Durham. I loved walking through the medieval streets of the city. Unlike the other kids, I wasn't so interested in all the cool shops or hanging around the shopping centre's new extension. Instead, I spent my time exploring the indoor market, wandering around the streets and visiting the cathedral. I would climb the 325 steps and just spend ages looking down on the city, daydreaming and imagining what it would have been like living there in the Middle Ages. Other times, I would take a walk over Elvet Bridge and peer over the wall to watch the rowing boats glide up and down the river.*

*Eventually, curiosity got the better of me and I managed to persuade a few of my mates to give rowing a try. We made our way down to the riverbank to hire a couple of wooden boats and set off on a wee adventure. We were just a bunch of kids having a laugh and messing about. We had no idea what we were doing, but I just loved being on the water. We had intended to row down to the cathedral – I had heard how amazing the views were from so low down on the water and was desperate to see for myself. The reality was, those boats are really hard to paddle! I think we managed to go a kilometre in the wrong direction, spinning around more than going forwards.*

*Those who know me may now understand why I get lost so often in my races. Navigation has never been my strong suit! However, there was something special and unique to me about being on the water. I didn't realise then that I was destined to spend most of my time on water in later life. Fast-forward a few years and with my Northern SUP teammates, I got to realise my little ambition of seeing those spectacular views from the river.*

# CUMBRIA

Cumbria is a paradise for paddlers, offering some of the most stunning and varied waterways in England. Known for its dramatic landscapes, Cumbria is home to the iconic Lake District National Park, a UNESCO World Heritage Site celebrated for its tranquil lakes, rugged fells and charming villages. For paddlers, this region provides an unrivalled blend of natural beauty and adventure.

The lakes themselves are the heart of Cumbria's paddling experience. Windermere, the largest natural lake in England, offers miles of open water, perfect for leisurely exploration. Derwentwater and Coniston Water provide a more serene setting, surrounded by towering peaks and dotted with accessible islands. Each lake has its own unique character, from the vast expanses of Ullswater to the secluded beauty of Wast Water.

I could write an entire book dedicated solely to the beauty of Cumbria and the Lake District. In this guide, I've focused on some of my favourite paddle spots, including quieter, lesser-known paddle places to help escape the crowds.

Beyond the water, Cumbria's historic and cultural significance enhances every paddling journey. Gliding across the same lakes that inspired Wordsworth's poetry or climbing iconic peaks that dominate the skyline creates a unique sense of connection to nature and history.

Whether you're a beginner seeking calm waters or an experienced paddler looking for adventure, Cumbria's waterways promise a truly unforgettable experience. It's a region where nature, history and the spirit of exploration converge to create a paddling destination like no other.

ABOVE Bruce paddling from Keswick to Grange (credit Simon Abram).

RIGHT Looking towards Lodore Falls.

# 11

# CARLISLE TO ROCKCLIFFE

The River Eden originates in the picturesque Eden Valley, winding its way north-west for 145km. It flows through the historic city of Carlisle before emptying into the Solway Firth. With its fast, shallow sections, this one-way paddle offers an exciting and dynamic adventure.

## The Lowdown

**DIFFICULTY**

**WATER TYPE**  River

**DISTANCE**  12km (one way)

**PARKING**  Swifts Bank car park

**WHAT3WORDS**  ///put.stir.cars

**LAUNCH**  Riverside

BELOW Rockcliffe at high tide.

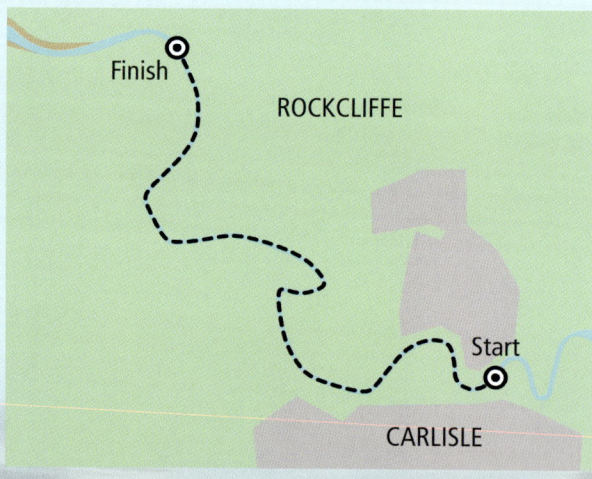

Finish

ROCKCLIFFE

Start

CARLISLE

## A brief history

Founded as Luguvalium by the Romans around AD 72, Carlisle served as a key support base for Hadrian's Wall and helped protect the northern frontier. Carlisle Castle was originally built as a wooden fortress in 1092, during the reign of William II, and was rebuilt in stone in 1122. The castle has witnessed many bloody battles throughout British history, and was designated a Scheduled Ancient Monument in 1996. An interesting fact about Carlisle is that Her Majesty's Theatre was one of the first theatres in the UK to be lit by electricity, achieving this milestone in 1880.

## The paddle

With the faster flowing water, this is a one-way paddle, finishing in a remote village, so you will need to arrange a pick-up or shuttle run with two vehicles.

Park in Swifts Bank car park and take a short walk along the footpath, which brings you to the riverbank, where a set of steps leads down to the water. The access point is in a slight eddy, allowing an easy launch. Once you push off, you'll quickly find yourself in the faster current, heading towards the stone arches of Eden Bridge. Designed by Robert Smirke and built in 1815, Eden Bridge connects the city of Carlisle with Stanwix.

After passing under the bridge, the flow slows and you are treated to a meandering tree-lined river. The water remains quite shallow, so keep an eye out for any submerged obstacles as you continue your journey downstream.

As you pass under the rail bridge after 2km, you may start to hear the rushing water of a short Grade II rapid located 500m further downstream. As you approach, there are several small beaches on the right-hand side. This is a great spot to pull in and assess the conditions. The rapid is usually straightforward to paddle through, but if you prefer you can easily portage around it and re-enter the water on the other side of the old Eden Viaduct.

If you stop here, take a moment to look across the river – you'll see the remains of the old Carlisle Canal wall. The canal, which once linked Carlisle to the Solway Firth, was very popular but short-lived, soon replaced by the railway network.

Although it may not have felt like you were paddling through a city, you soon pass under the Carlisle bypass road bridge. From here, the river winds through 8km of open

countryside, offering a peaceful stretch of river before reaching Rockcliffe. With the ever-changing riverbed, there could be shallow – Grade I at most – rapids or temporary islands appearing in the river.

After 11km, you'll approach the village of Rockcliffe on the right, with its church spire rising above the treetops. Look out for a detached house set back and an upturned white boat in the field next to the water. This marks the easiest exit point. Take care when landing, as at lower water levels it can be quite slippery. Once off the water, cross over the field to the small car park, completing this memorable journey.

## Wildlife
Expect to see plenty of **Atlantic salmon** leaping from October through to December. Look out for **otters** by the riverbank; **herons**, **cormorants** and **kingfishers** are also regularly seen.

## Food stops
• **The Crown & Thistle** in Rockcliffe is a traditional country pub offering a menu packed with homemade food using locally sourced produce. Dog-friendly, with a log fire and a cosy atmosphere, it's a perfect place for a post-paddle meal.
• **The Turf Tavern**, located to the rear of the launch car park, is a family-friendly Hungry Horse pub serving food and drinks from 11am to 9pm seven days a week.
• **Adeline's Tea Room** on Corporation Road, Carlisle, is a quaint little tearoom serving a wide variety of cakes, sweet treats and light bites.

## Getting there
• **By car** – From the A69, turn on to Georgian Way. Turn right at the roundabout into Newmarket Road and follow to Swifts Bank car park.

## NEED TO KNOW
■ This is a fast-moving river with banksides that are ever changing. Be aware of sandbanks and hidden branches or trees that could have been washed downstream.

■ There are no toilets in the car park. However, toilets are available if using The Turf Tavern opposite the car park.

■ River fins are advisable.

• **By train** – The nearest train station is Carlisle, on the West Coast Main Line. The station is a 15-minute walk to the launch spot.
• **By bus** – The nearest bus stop is Carlisle bus station, a 10-minute walk away.

## Other activities
• **Carlisle Castle** has stood proud in the city for nine centuries. It remained a working fortress until well within living memory. Now owned by English Heritage, this medieval castle is well worth a visit.
• **Hadrian's Wall**, the largest Roman archaeological feature in Britain, stretching 117km from Bowness-on-Solway in the west to Wallsend in the east, passes right through the city of Carlisle. It's a popular long-distance walk and cycle route. The longest continuous remaining stretch of wall can be found just outside **Birdoswald Roman Fort**.

ABOVE The calm River Eden.

RIGHT The old bridge abutment.

# 12 RIVER DERWENT – GRANGE TO DERWENTWATER

The crystal-clear waters of the River Derwent provide a great introduction to moving water. The short Grade I rapids provide some thrills, while the majestic calm waters allow you to soak up all the breathtaking scenery the Lake District National Park has to offer.

## The Lowdown

**DIFFICULTY** 🌢🌢 to 🌢🌢🌢

**WATER TYPE** River and lake

**DISTANCE** 5km (round trip)

**PARKING** Car park

**WHAT3WORDS** ///cinemas.teardrop.surfacing

**LAUNCH** Bankside

## A brief history

Originally established in the 13th century as a monastic farm managed by Furness Abbey, Grange derives its name from the old French word grange, meaning granary. The village gradually expanded, and in 1675 the distinctive double-arched stone bridge was built. Today, Grange is a quaint tourist destination that retains an unspoiled charm.

## The paddle

Park in the small car park just over the bridge and follow the path down to the river. If the water level is low then you may have a short walk along the shingle to reach deeper water. The first 1km of this paddle features a

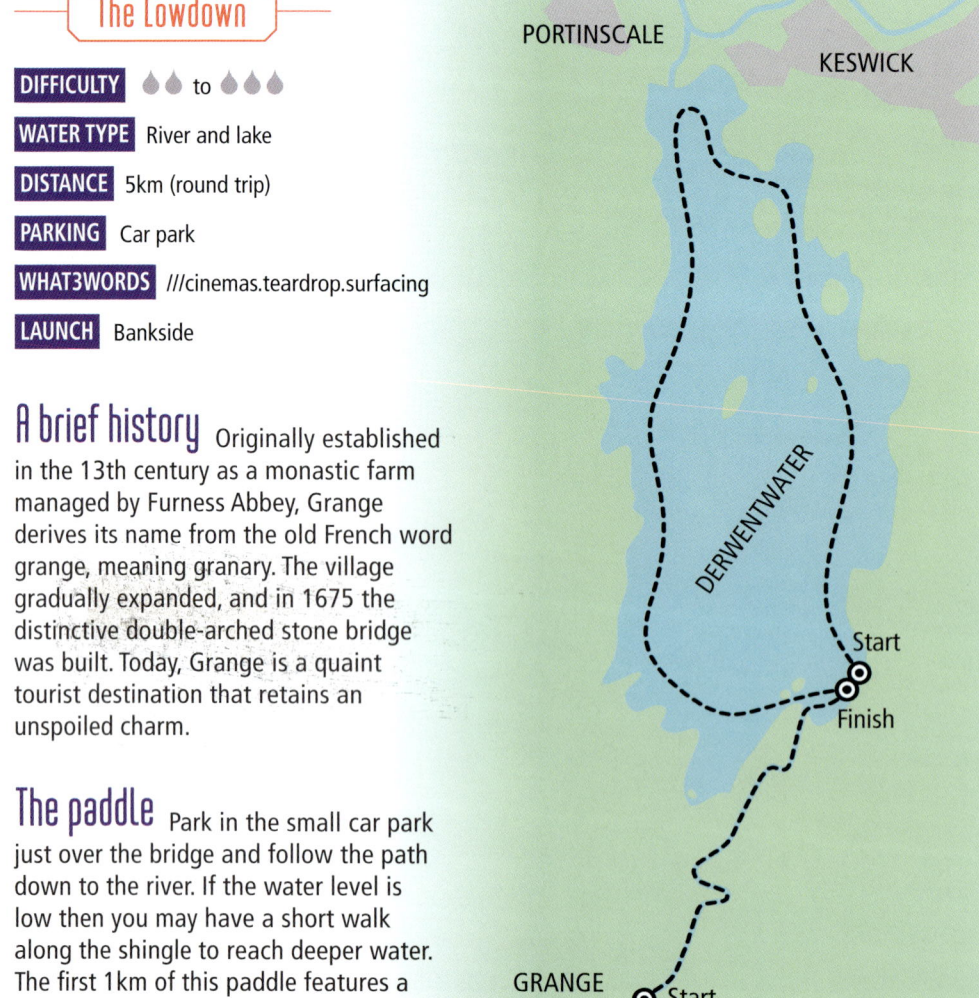

RIGHT Bruce paddling from Keswick to Grange (credit Simon Abram).

mix of deeper sections that soon change to very shallow water, so a river fin is a 'must-have' on this paddle. The crystal-clear water, however, makes it very easy to see the changes in depth. Some of the shallow water leads to slight Grade I rapids, but they last no more than 20 or 30m. As you wind your way through the trees and open fields, you'll enjoy stunning views of the Derwent Hills.

After 1.5km, you pass under a footbridge and soon the river deepens for the rest of the paddle to Derwentwater. Upon reaching the lake, you have several options. To the right is Kettlewell car park, (///exact.depths.passages), located next to a nice gentle sloping beach. This is a good starting point if you prefer to do the paddle in reverse. However, note that the car park has a height restriction barrier of only 1.6m, making it unsuitable for vans or cars with a roof box.

There are few restrictions to paddling on Derwentwater. Derwent Isle and Lord's Island are off-limits, but feel free to pull up and explore St Herbert's Island, Rampsholme Island or any of the smaller ones dotted around the lake. As always on large, open bodies of water, be mindful: the weather conditions can change quickly.

On the return paddle, the adventure continues. The slow-moving water allows you to take in more breathtaking views of the 'Jaws of Borrowdale', Castle Crag and Grange Fell. As you move further up the river and reach the shallow water, it can be easier to step off the board and walk a few paces until it is deep enough to clear the fin again. The riverbed is mainly made up of small pebbles and shale, so it isn't too challenging underfoot, but good footwear is recommended. It's not too long before Grange Bridge comes into view. Exit the water on the right-hand side and follow the footpath back to the car park.

## Wildlife

While looking up at the views, keep an eye out for **red kites** soaring above. Down at water level, keep your eyes open for **dippers** searching for food around the shallow water.

## Food stops

• **The Grange Café** serves an amazing Cumberland breakfast as well as a variety of hot and cold sandwiches, snacks and hot and cold drinks.

• **Mizu Pan Asian Restaurant**, located in the Lodore Falls Hotel & Spa, serves the best of Japanese, Korean, Chinese, Vietnamese and Thai cuisine.

## Getting there

• **By car** – From Keswick, head south on the B5289 for 5km. Turn right over the bridge into Grange and the car park is on your right-hand side.

• **By train** – The nearest train station is Penrith on the West Coast Main Line (35km).

ABOVE Derwentwater to Grange (credit Simon Abram).

RIGHT Grange bridge.

BELOW The silky water of the River Derwent looking towards Grange.

• **By bus** – The Borrowdale Bus 78 runs from Keswick and stops just outside Grange.

## Other activities

It goes without saying that the Lake District is a haven for walkers, but **Ashness Bridge**, **Surprise View** and **Lodore Falls** are definitely worth checking out on foot. Also head to the **Bowder Stone**, a 2,000-ton boulder that fell from Kings How 10,000 years ago, and climb the metal ladder leading to the top of this impressive landmark.

## NEED TO KNOW

■ There are several shallow sections on this paddle so wear appropriate footwear and be prepared to make a couple of short walks through the water.

■ The river is prone to flooding so always check local forecasts before you set off on your paddle.

■ Toilets are available in Grange for a small (50p) charge.

## ANECDOTE FROM THE RIVER DERWENT

My early memories of trips to the Lake District almost always included a visit to Grange. In fact, my first ever camping trip was with the Boys' Brigade. I must have been about 14 years old, and we spent a week camped by the River Derwent, enjoying team-building games and swimming in the river. Some of the older kids brought some rope and rigged up a makeshift zipline between the trees across the river. We would slide down at breakneck speed and midway across, we had to let go and land in the water. The incentive to let go? Avoiding the alternative – crashing into the tree trunk at the other side! It was great fun, and I couldn't get enough of the adrenaline rush. I can't imagine it being approved by health and safety these days!

Another day was spent hiking up the nearby Castle Crag. Alfred Wainwright admired its majestic appearance so much he included it in his Pictorial Guide to the Lakeland Fells. Although it stands less than 1,000 feet, it felt to me like I'd climbed Mount Everest. Standing on the summit, taking in the views down towards Derwentwater, I knew I wanted my life to involve mountains and water. On returning home from that trip, I constantly badgered my parents to return. And return we did, many times.

When my son, Ben, was nine, I decided it was time to introduce him to the wonders of Grange and its 'mountain'. He was full of enthusiasm to climb a real mountain, and all was going well until we rounded a corner halfway up. He just froze, hugging the inside slate wall. He refused to budge and there was nothing I could do, so back down we went. Five minutes later, he turned to me and said, 'Dad, can I try again?' So off we went, heading back up. It was all good until we reached the same spot and once again, he froze! This scene was repeated another four times! Each time he was becoming braver, until he just ran round the bend and that was it. He kept going, me chasing behind him until he reached the top.

The joy on his face as he looked out from the summit said it all. I didn't need to say anything, it brought me back to the day I conquered Castle Crag. It was, without question, my proudest Dad moment ever.

# 13 ULLSWATER

**Stretching 11km in length, 1km in width, and reaching a depth of 63m,** Ullswater is the second largest lake in the region. The extenuated Z-shaped ribbon lake provides endless opportunities for paddling, from calm sheltered water to an exhilarating downwind run along its length. Whatever the weather, there is always somewhere to enjoy a paddle on this most picturesque lake.

## The Lowdown

**DIFFICULTY**  ⬤⬤⬤

**WATER TYPE**  Lake

**DISTANCE**  Variable:
  **3km Norfolk Island** (round trip)
  **8km to Howtown** (one way)
  **12km to Pooley Bridge** (one way)

**PARKING**  Ullswater Steamers car park

**WHAT3WORDS**  ///disarmed.achieving.lunch

**LAUNCH**  Shingle beach

## A brief history

Ullswater was formed during the last Ice Age when three glaciers converged, sculpting the valley floor into its distinctive shape. Paddle steamers have been sailing on the lake for almost 200 years, originally transporting passengers, post, provisions, slate and lead from the mines above Glenridding. In 1955, Donald Campbell set a water speed world record

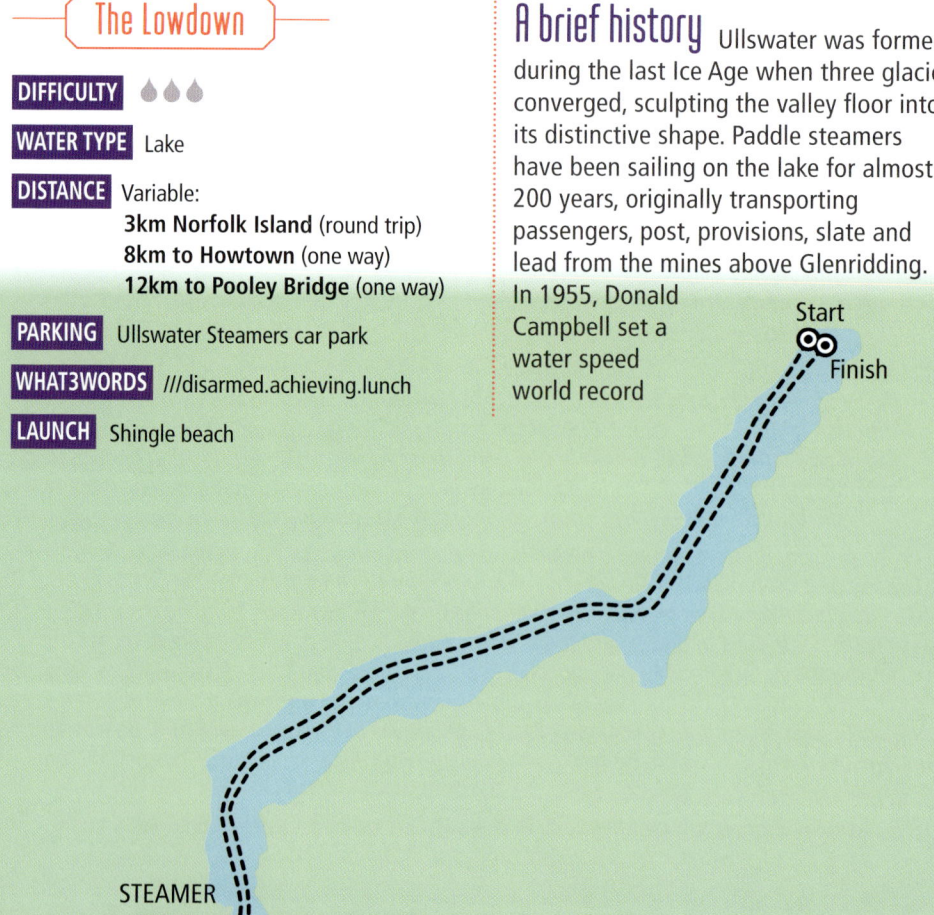

Start
Finish

STEAMER
FERRY

on Ullswater in his iconic *Bluebird K7*. The fully restored K7 is now on display in the Ruskin Museum in Coniston.

## The paddle

Park in the Ullswater Steamers car park and launch from the beach just to the left of the steamer pier. This area is often lively, especially in summer, with frequent steamers and dinghies from the sailing club located on the spit of land next to the pier, so stay vigilant to steer clear of incoming and outgoing boats. Once on the water, head north towards Pooley Bridge. After 500m you reach the small island of Wall Holm; another kilometre brings you to Norfolk Island. This makes an ideal stopping point for a picnic while taking in Ullswater's iconic backdrop of rolling hills. For those looking for a shorter paddle, you can return to Glenridding from here to make a rewarding 3km round trip.

ABOVE The Inn on the Lake Hotel.

As you continue north, the lake starts to bear right and marks the first of two main kinks in this beautiful ribbon lake. Depending on the day's wind conditions you may notice the texture of the water shifting, so always be aware of any changes to the weather. About 1.5km from Norfolk Island, you'll come across Aira Point, where a narrow spit of land juts into the lake on your left. For those seeking a little more adventure, you can beach your craft here and take a short trek up to the famous Aira Force waterfall, a stunning spot with a 20m cascade surrounded by beautiful woodland. After 7km, the lake bends left again; if you decide you're ready for home then veer right and head towards Howtown to catch the steamer back to the car park. If carrying on to Pooley Bridge, keep an eye out for Dunmallard Hill ahead – a tree-covered vantage point and the landmark of your

destination. As you approach Pooley Bridge, the steamer pier and north shoreline are private, so head to the beach just before the stone jetty on the right. You can exit the water here and follow the path into Pooley Bridge, where cafés and pubs make for a well-earned rest, before catching the steamer back to Glenridding.

## Wildlife

As you paddle along the shoreline, you may be lucky to spot a **Martindale red deer**, one of Britain's oldest native herds. Endangered **red squirrels** are also hiding among the woodland. On the water, expect to see **lapwings**, **cormorants** and **ospreys**.

## Food stops

• **Helvellyn Country Kitchen** in Glenridding serves freshly prepared homemade dishes and delicious cakes.
• **Granny Dowbekin's Cafe & Restaurant** in Pooley Bridge pride themselves on their menu full of family favourites, using locally sourced produce.

## Getting there

• **By car** – Glenridding is on the A592. Turn into Ullswater Steamers and the car park is situated at the lakeside.
• **By train** – The nearest train station is Penrith on the West Coast Main Line or TransPennine Express services.
• **By bus** – Stagecoach buses run from Penrith train stain to Ullswater Steamers. On weekends and bank holidays from 31 March to 2 November you can catch the 509 bus, which runs between Penrith and Keswick.

## Other activities

• From Glenridding, you can **hike to the summit of Helvellyn**; at 950m, it is England's third highest peak. Always ensure

you are fully prepared with the appropriate clothing, nutrition and experience before hiking in the Lake District.
• **Aira Force waterfall**, with its impressive 20m drop, is well worth a visit. Take time to explore the **woodland trails** that wind up to Gowbarrrow Fell summit, an ideal spot to see the views over Ullswater. Along the way, you may also spot a rare red squirrel.

## NEED TO KNOW

■ Several toilets are available in the car park.

■ The weather in the Lake District can be unpredictable. Always keep a close eye on what the weather is doing and wear appropriate clothing.

TOP The view of Ullswater from the north shore.

ABOVE Anna with Alison and Allistair on a tandem SUP at Ullswater (credit Daniel Godridge).

# 14 ST BEES

**The most westerly point in northern England,** St Bees provides an exhilarating adventure along the rugged Cumbrian coast. Navigate beneath the towering red sandstone cliffs, home to an array of seabirds, before arriving at the secluded Fleswick Bay. This paddle is a perfect blend of natural beauty and wildlife.

## The Lowdown

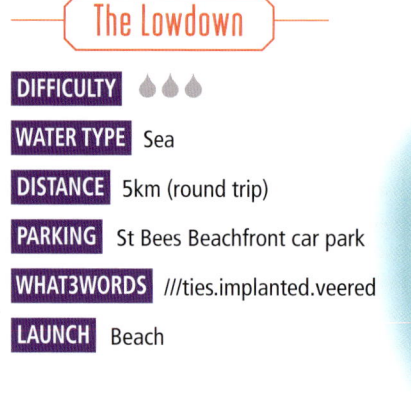

**DIFFICULTY** ⬤⬤⬤

**WATER TYPE** Sea

**DISTANCE** 5km (round trip)

**PARKING** St Bees Beachfront car park

**WHAT3WORDS** ///ties.implanted.veered

**LAUNCH** Beach

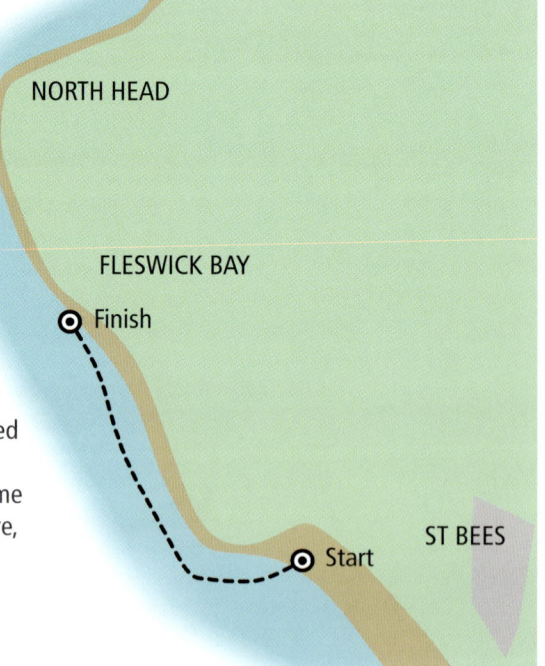

**A brief history** The village of St Bees can trace its origins to the 7th century, when it is said the Irish saint Bega founded a nunnery. A Benedictine priory was established in the 12th century and became a significant religious and economic centre, with the monks working the land, fishing the sea and extending the buildings. The priory closed in the 16th century with the dissolution of the monasteries by Henry VIII. The nave of the priory continues in use today as the parish church.

The arrival of the railway to the village in 1849 catalysed significant local development, facilitating the quarrying and transport of red sandstone, much of which was used in the construction of Barrow-in-Furness. The railway also made the village accessible for tourists who had previously visited Whitehaven and Workington. Today, St Bees attracts numerous visitors and hikers each year, eager to embark on Alfred Wainwright's famous Coast to Coast walk.

Wainwright selected the village for its dramatic and stunning coastal landscape as the starting point for this renowned long-distance trek.

## The paddle

Launch from the sandy St Bees beach. A good time to start the paddle is an hour before high tide, when it's nice and tranquil to move out from the beach. Leave the shore towards the red sandstone cliffs, which tower above you. You may not want to get too close to the rocks at the base of the cliffs as the sea can start to get chopped up from any swells rebounding off the cliff walls. On a clear, calm day, it is possible to make out the Isle of Man on the horizon out to the left. As you make your way along the coastline, keep an eye out for the secluded cove of Fleswick Bay nestled into the base of the cliffs. When approaching the beach, take extra care to avoid hitting any submerged rocks. After enjoying a little picnic on the beach, where you can take in the seabirds and spot dolphins, return down the coastline to St Bees.

## Wildlife

The red sandstone cliffs are a nature reserve and home to England's only colony of **black guillemots**. You can also see **razorbills**, **puffins**, **terns** and **kittiwakes** among the many **gulls** nesting in the cliffs. While out on the water, also keep an eye out for **dolphins** and **harbour porpoises**, which regularly pass by, particularly during July to September.

## Food stops

• **Beach Road Bakehouse**, located adjacent to Seacote Beach car park, champions locally sourced ingredients. It serves high-quality homemade breakfasts, light lunches and cakes. It is in a prime location with its views over the sea and St Bees Head.
• **The Manor Inn**, located in the village, is a traditional pub serving classic homemade pub food and ales.

## Getting there

• **By car** – From the M6 Penrith junction, take the A66 to Cockermouth then the A595 to Whitehaven. From Whitehaven, follow local signs to St Bees.
• **By train** – St Bees station, on the Cumbrian Coast Line between Carlisle and

BELOW Groynes along St Bees beach (credit Tracey Laing).

Barrow-in-Furness, is situated in the centre of the village. If you are travelling from Carlisle, check timetables as some trains terminate at Whitehaven.

• **By bus** – There is no direct bus to St Bees. The nearest bus stop is in Whitehaven, where you can then take either a taxi or the train, which is a journey of around 8 minutes.

## Other activities

• If the thought of walking Wainwright's 306km to **Robin Hood's Bay** is a little too much, why not follow the route up over the cliffs, heading to Fleswick Bay for some bird-spotting.
• **St Bees Priory** is located in the heart of the village. It's open to visitors seven days a week.

## NEED TO KNOW

■ Toilet facilities are available in the car park.

■ This is a challenging sea paddle and the water can get very choppy. Always wear appropriate clothing and safety equipment.

■ Always check the weather conditions and tides. This paddle is best suited to neap tides and very low winds.

• **The Cumbrian Coast Express** runs steam train excursions along the Cumbrian coast and through the Lake District.

ABOVE Looking towards St Bees Head.

BELOW Looking down from the coastal path.

# 15 WAST WATER

Located in Wasdale, a valley in the western part of the Lake District National Park, Wast Water is a ribbon lake nearly 5km long and 500m wide and, with a depth of 79m, is England's deepest lake. It's surrounded by the mountains of Yewbarrow, Kirk Fell, Great Gable and England's highest, Scafell Pike. From the highest mountain to the deepest lake, Wast Water is an awe-inspiring place to paddle, with a jaw-dropping view.

## The Lowdown

**DIFFICULTY** 🌢🌢 to 🌢🌢🌢 depending on weather

**WATER TYPE** Lake

**DISTANCE** 9km (circumference)

**PARKING** Lay-bys along the shoreline

**WHAT3WORDS** ///migrate.plump.quilt

**LAUNCH** Shoreline

## A brief history

This is another of the Lake District's famous glacial ribbon lakes, formed 10,000 years ago at the end of the last Ice Age. The name derives from the Norse word 'Vatin', meaning water. Unlike other areas of the Lake District, the Wasdale Valley has been pretty much left undisturbed from development over the years. The only access road is the single-track lane from western Cumbria leading up to Wasdale Head, resulting in an unspoiled landscape free from the touristy feel of other areas in this national park.

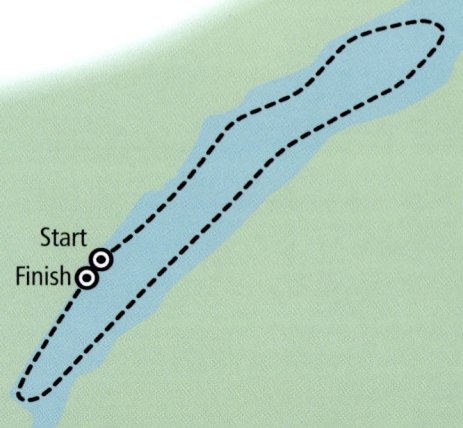

Start
Finish

# The paddle

Access to the water can be found from the many lay-bys along the road that runs the length of the western shore. I like to use the small parking area near Countess Beck. As the road is single track, please ensure that you park in a designated parking lay-by and not a passing place. Although Wast Water is one of the quieter areas of the Lake District, the lay-bys can fill up quickly so it is always good to get there early. Some of the access spots are from smooth shingle beaches, others are more stony, so I would recommend always wearing footwear when entering the water. After a couple of metres, the lake-bed soon drops into deep water.

Once on the water, head in a north-easterly direction towards Wasdale Head, taking in the breathtaking sight of Britain's favourite view, as voted by viewers of ITV. Looking ahead, you have Yewbarrow on the left, Great Gable in the centre and the Scafell range to the right. Paddling up Wast Water can take me a very long time as I can't help just standing or sitting on my board, dangling my feet in the water and absorbing the surrounding vistas.

Approaching the end of the lake, there is another beach, perfect for a picnic and watching the alpacas from Wastwater Alpaca Trekking grazing the land. On a calm day, I like to return down the eastern side, where I truly get a sense of the scale of the scree slopes towering above. It's a little under 5km down towards the youth hostel, so always be aware of any change in the weather as there are no beaches or get-out places. There is, however, a small public footpath that traverses the lower screes. It's not for the faint-hearted, but I have seen small flocks of Herdwick sheep walking along the perilous slope. As you reach the southern end of the lake, the valley flattens out at Low Wood, and you can just make out Wasdale Hall youth hostel nestled among the trees. If you are staying in the hostel, you also have permission to access the lake from there. From here, it's only a kilometre back to Countess Beck.

# Wildlife

The brown-bodied, white-headed **Herdwick sheep** native to the Lake District have adapted to survive the extreme weather conditions the Lake District can bring and have been known to survive for days under a blanket of snow eating only their own wool. If you look up into the sky, it's possible to spot **buzzards** soaring above.

# Food stops

• **The Wasdale Head Inn** to the north of the lake is popular with walkers heading up or returning from climbing Scafell Pike. It serves classic pub grub, fine ales and wines.
• **The Screes Inn** to the south of the lake pride themselves on meals made from locally sourced ingredients. They serve beers from their own microbrewery.

BELOW Yewbarrow, Great Gable and Lingmell from Wast Water.

## Getting there

• **By car** – Wast Water can be accessed from the west by following the A595 from Gosforth, picking up signs for Wasdale. Follow the narrow lane until reaching the water.

• **By train** – Ravenglass train station is on the Cumbrian Coast Line. The shuttle bus picks up from here during the summer months (see below).

• **By bus** – There is a shuttle bus that runs on weekends and bank holidays during the summer months. Check www.lakedistrict.gov.uk for an up-to-date timetable and destinations.

## Other activities

• **St Olaf's** at Wasdale Head is England's smallest parish church.

• **Carolclimb** run climbing and mountaineering lessons and excursions around Wasdale. Details can be found on their website: www.carolclimb.co.uk.

• **Muncaster Castle** and gardens near Ravenglass is a historic house with attractions for all the family. During the summer months, the Wasdale shuttle bus picks up here.

ABOVE Karen paddling towards Wasdale Head with Scafell Pike coming into view.

## NEED TO KNOW

■ There are no toilet or changing facilities along the shoreline. There is a National Trust car park at Lake Head beach with a small toilet block nearby.

■ The water temperature can get very cold even in the summer, so always wear appropriate clothing.

■ The weather can be very unpredictable in the mountains and the glass-like water can soon change to a windy, bumpy, sea-like state. Always check local weather forecasts and if in any doubt leave this one for another day.

# 16 CONISTON WATER

At 8km long, 800m wide, and with a maximum depth of 56m, Coniston Water is the fifth largest lake by area in the Lake District. Lying beneath the towering backdrop of the Old Man of Coniston, the tranquil waters of Coniston have been and are still used today for many water speed world record attempts. With the obvious exception of the annual Power Boats Record Week, Coniston Water offers plenty of opportunities for paddling.

## The Lowdown

**DIFFICULTY** 💧💧💧

**WATER TYPE** Lake

**DISTANCE** 13.5km (round trip)

**PARKING** Monk Coniston car park

**WHAT3WORDS** ///seatbelt.stubborn.pretty

**LAUNCH** Beach

## A brief history

Originally named Thorstein's Water after the Norse invader who settled in the valley and asserted ownership of the lake-bed, it wasn't until the late 18th century that it was renamed Coniston Water.

Coniston Water is probably best known for the many water speed world records that have been set here. In 1939, Sir Malcolm Campbell set the record of 141.74 miles per hour.

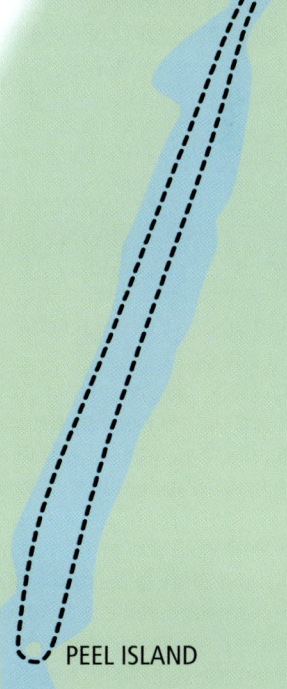

MONK CONISTON CAR PARK

CONISTON

Start

Finish

PEEL ISLAND

His son, Donald Campbell, followed in his footsteps, setting four more world records on Coniston until one fateful day in January 1967 when, attempting to push his turbo jet-engined hydroplane *Bluebird K7* to over 300 miles per hour, his plane flipped over, killing him instantly. *Bluebird K7* has since been recovered and fully restored, and is on display in the Ruskin Museum in the village.

## The paddle

**Paddle 1: Monk Coniston – Peel Island**
Access to the water is from the sheltered pebble beach directly opposite the car park. The beach slopes gently for the first couple of metres with a few scattered larger rocks, so just be a little careful with your fin as you enter the water. Head off in a southerly direction towards Peel Island.

After the first kilometre, Coniston Boating Centre can be seen on the westerly side. This is also the launch site for the National Trust steam yacht *Gondola*.

Continuing down the lake, on the eastern bankside are numerous beaches. If you are feeling tired, or you don't want to paddle the full route, or you just want a little break and time to take in the breathtaking scenery, there is a small road running alongside.

Soon, Peel Island can be seen up ahead. It was the inspiration for Arthur Ransome's Wild Cat Island in his book *Swallows and Amazons* and was also featured in W.G. Collingwood's *Thorstein of the Mere: A Saga of the Northmen in Lakeland*. As you go around the island there is a small hidden natural harbour where you can land, stretch your legs and explore this little gem.

Once back on the water and returning to the start point, the views of the Old Man of Coniston are quite spectacular. No matter how many times I paddle here, I love to take the time to sit with my feet dangling in the water, staring in wonderment at its beauty.

**Paddle 2: Rigg Wood – Peel Island**
If you are still looking to explore Peel Island but would prefer a shorter paddle, there is a launch spot at Rigg Wood (///tester.narrowest.customers) on the east bank. This is around 500m one way. Brown Howe car park is on the south-west bank and is 1km away (///removes.represent.whom).

## Wildlife
Although they may be almost impossible to spot, it is interesting to know that relic fish from the Ice Age, the **Arctic charr,** are swimming below the water. Closer to the surface, playing along the shoreline, you may see a family of **otters**. You will also see many **cormorants, mallard ducks** and **geese** on the water.

## Food stops
The dog-friendly **Bluebird Café** is situated on the shoreline next to the steam yacht *Gondola* and offers freshly prepared food, homemade cakes, ice cream and a good selection of beers and wine.

ABOVE Boat house.

LEFT The fells above Coniston.

## Getting there

• **By car** – Coniston is towards the southern end of the Lake District. Take the A593 from Ambleside then the B5285, which takes you to Monk Coniston car park.
• **By train** – The nearest train stations are Windermere and Haverthwaite.
• **By bus** – The nearest bus stop is Monk Coniston Hall. Take the 505 bus from Coniston or Hawshead. There are also bus stops in Coniston village.

## Other activities

• Check out the **Ruskin Museum** and learn more about Donald Campbell and Coniston's full history, from the Stone Age fell-walkers to the present day.
• For avid experienced hikers and walkers, you can reach the 'Tourist Route' that takes you to the top of the **Old Man of Coniston** (803m). This is a challenging route, and the appropriate clothing and equipment is needed. There are small single-track roads running along both sides of the lake for those wishing to do a less strenuous walk.
• It is well worth taking a trip across the lake in the **National Trust Steam Yacht Gondola**, a restored Victorian yacht. Tickets can be booked in advance through the National Trust website: www.nationaltrust.org.uk.

## NEED TO KNOW

■ The weather on Coniston can be very unpredictable so be sure to check local forecasts before heading out to paddle.

■ Toilets are available at the car park; however, they are closed throughout the winter.

# 17 LAKE WINDERMERE

'I overlooked the bed of Windermere. Like a vast river, stretching in the sun. With exultation, at my feet I saw lake, islands, promontories, gleaming bays, a universe of Nature's fairest forms. Proudly revealed with instantaneous burst. Magnificent, and beautiful, and gay.' Lake Windermere's beauty was the inspiration for William Wordsworth's poem 'Summer Vacation'. Now a mecca for watersports and outdoor enthusiasts alike, Windermere offers an abundance of paddle opportunities. At 17km long and 1.6km wide, it's England's largest and busiest lake.

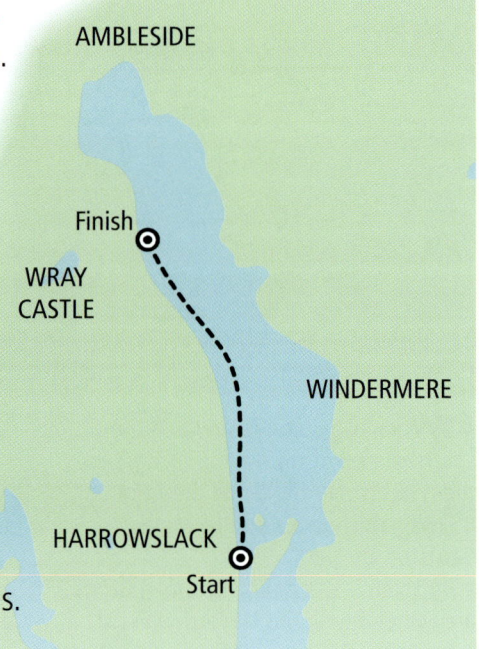

AMBLESIDE

Finish

WRAY CASTLE

WINDERMERE

HARROWSLACK

Start

## The Lowdown

**DIFFICULTY** ▲ to ▲▲▲ depending on routes and weather

**WATER TYPE** Lake/river

**DISTANCE** 10km/3km (round trip)

**PARKING** Lay-by/car park

**WHAT3WORDS** ///loves.respond.allowable ///blaze.fracture.blotchy

**LAUNCH** Beach/jetty

## A brief history
It's not only Loch Ness that lays claim to a monster of the deep. A glacially carved ribbon lake formed during the Ice Age, Lake Windermere is reported to hide its very own mysterious creature of the deep: Bownessie. There have been many reported sightings of the elusive beast, named after the local town of Bowness.

# The paddle

## Paddle 1: Harrowslack to the Islands and Wray Castle (10km)

My preferred parking spot is a small car park half a kilometre up from the larger Harrowslack car park (free for National Trust members) as it is right beside the lake. There is limited parking and does fill up pretty quickly, so it's best to get there early. From the beach aim for the group of islands opposite the launch point. The largest of these, Belle Island (see map right), is privately owned, so landing is prohibited. You are allowed to land on the others and explore to your heart's content If you are looking for a shorter paddle, then return back to Harrowslack.

If you want a longer paddle, leave the islands and head north up the lake towards Wray Castle (see map left). Away from the more sheltered waters of the islands, the water can get quite choppy from the motorboats, lake cruises and other powered craft allowed on Windermere; it can feel very exposed the further out you go, so it is better to keep closer to the shoreline. Soon, you pass the quaint little house in front of Strawberry Gardens Caravan Site, which is hidden in the trees. After 3km you arrive at

Red Nab car park. There is a small beach to the side, making it an easy stop here to rest and enjoy a snack before continuing your journey. Once past the car park, the magnificent Wray Castle emerges into sight, gradually revealing itself from the trees. It's possible to land on the beach and walk 300m up to the castle.

## Paddle 2: Newby Bridge – Fell Foot (3km)

Begin your journey at Newby Bridge, accessing the River Leven from the northern side of the bridge, either from the low wall or the jetty adjacent to the Swan Hotel. The river can be quite shallow at first

BELOW The River Leven from Fell Foot.

but soon deepens as you make your way towards Fell Foot. Follow the river around to the right and then left before reaching the start of Lake Windermere, where Fell Foot Park can be seen on your right-hand side. Once on the lake, it's worth paddling the 500m further up to see the Windermere steamers and Lakeside railway station before making your way over to Fell Foot Park and returning downstream to Newby Bridge. Avoid passing beneath the bridge, as the water accelerates towards a weir on the far side.

Paid parking is available in the Swan Hotel car park, refundable if you spend £10 in the hotel.

## Wildlife

The rare **pochard** is a regular visitor to the lake, while on land there is a large colony of **red squirrels**. If you're lucky, you may see **red** and **roe deer** through the trees.

## Food stops

• **Joey's Café** at Claife Viewing Station is a plant-based café serving a wide variety of hot and cold snacks.
• **Lake View Garden Bar** in Windermere is dog-friendly and has excellent views of the lake and hills.

## Getting there

• **By car** – Harrowslack car park is on the west shore and can be reached via the Wray-Windermere car and passenger ferry, then turn right onto the un-named road. Newby Bridge is at the southernmost end of the lake, just off the A590; then over the bridge and the launch spot is immediately on your right.
• **By train** – The nearest train station is Windermere.
• **By bus** – The nearest bus stops are in Windermere.

RIGHT Sharing the lake with the cruisers.

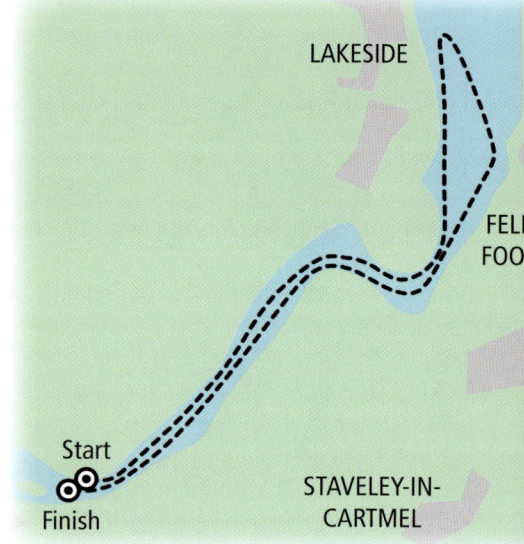

LAKESIDE

FELL FOOT

Start

Finish

STAVELEY-IN-CARTMEL

## Other activities

• Enjoy a leisurely ride on a steam train with the **Lakeside & Haverthwaite Railway**, taking in the breathtaking views along the Leven Valley.
• **Lakeland District Falconry** offer bespoke falconry experiences.

## NEED TO KNOW

■ The conditions can change very quickly on the lake so always check local weather forecasts.

■ Be aware of other water users, particularly the cruise boats; they kick out quite a lot of wake behind them.

■ There are no toilets or changing facilities at Harrowslack car park.

■ Toilets and changing facilities are available at Newby Bridge.

## ANECDOTE FROM WINDERMERE

*In June 2018, Karen and I found ourselves driving over to Windermere for the Summer Solstice Race hosted by Windermere Canoe Kayak. It's open to all kinds of paddle craft. On this occasion it was part of the GBSUP National series of races, and I was competing in the 'Nisco' category. Nisco is a one-design category where every competitor is on exactly the same board, which makes for a fair and even race. The boards used are the Naish One 'Nisco'; they are 12'6" x 30", making them a great choice not only for racing but also for an everyday SUP.*

*The drive over was filled with the usual mix of nerves and excitement. The race started at Waterhead, at the northern end of the lake, and ran the full 17km length to Fell Foot at the southern end. I had never paddled that distance before and genuinely didn't know if I could complete it!*

*At 11am I found myself lined up at the start along with around 20 other Nisco paddlers. With the width of the start, we all had enough space for a clean getaway. We had a slight tail wind, which I presumed would help get this race over quicker. How wrong could I be! The early part, although frantic, was quite enjoyable, but as I moved down the lake the bumps were building and were soon bigger than I had experienced before. All thoughts of being competitive were now out the window as I saw the leaders seemingly glide off into the distance. I remember thinking, the best way to learn is to race. I was having a ball trying to put into practice things I'd been told and videos I'd watched online.*

*Midway through the race, I guess I was getting to grips with the conditions, and realised I had made my way into fourth place; I managed to catch up to Deke Moran and we worked together through the middle section, swapping places and catching each other's drafts. We could see Simon Day up ahead, but always out of reach.*

*The winds had been swirling around and as we moved into the final third of the course, we were facing quite a strong headwind. This suited me fine, and I was now feeling right in my comfort zone so decided to try and make a move. Digging deep, shouting to Deke 'Come on, we can catch him', I soon found myself catching Simon and had the dilemma of drafting to recover or pushing on to Steve Rutt, who was out in front. I went with the latter and gave everything I had to reach him. I could tell he was tiring, and I was gaining fast! I could see the finish in the distance and for one moment I had hoped I could take him on the line. However, Steve is made of different stuff. He glanced around and saw me, then just powered on to cross the finish line in a well-deserved first place.*

*To this day, this remains one of my favourite races ever and something I'll never forget.*

# YORKSHIRE

Yorkshire, the largest historic county in England, is a region of immense variety, stretching from the rugged coastline of the North Sea to the rolling hills of the North York Moors, the Dales and the Pennines. Often labelled as 'God's Own Country', Yorkshire now even has its own celebration day each year. It's not surprising that it's also a paddlers' paradise, offering a mix of urban waterways, exciting rivers and scenic canals.

The striking white chalk cliffs along the coastline at Flamborough are another standout highlight of the region. With its sea caves, hidden coves and dramatic landscapes, this area provides thrilling adventures for both walkers and paddlers alike.

Yorkshire is also renowned for its long-distance walking routes, many of which intersect with its waterways. The Coast to Coast Path, the Cleveland Way and the Pennine Way offer opportunities to combine paddling with hiking, creating unique multi-activity journeys. These trails showcase the county's breathtaking landscapes and connect its charming towns and villages.

At the county's heart lies York, a gem of a city founded by the Romans and later shaped by Viking settlers. Paddling the River Ouse through York provides a unique perspective on its iconic landmarks, including the majestic York Minster and the ancient city walls. The combination of rich history and delightful riverside views makes it a truly unforgettable experience.

To the west, the UNESCO World Heritage Site of Saltaire stands as a testament to Yorkshire's industrial heritage. This model Victorian village, founded by Sir Titus Salt, sits along the Leeds & Liverpool Canal, offering paddlers the chance to glide past its impressive mill and picturesque landscapes.

Whether you're navigating through diverse cities, exploring scenic countryside or immersing yourself in the county's rich cultural heritage, Yorkshire offers a captivating blend of past and present. With its unique combination of dramatic natural beauty, notable landmarks and opportunities for adventure, Yorkshire truly stands out as an essential destination for water-based exploration.

ABOVE Karen and Tom on the River Tees.

RIGHT Runswick Bay from the sea.

# 18 SEMERWATER

A hidden beauty deep in the Yorkshire Dales, Semerwater is the perfect destination to reconnect with nature and escape the hustle and bustle. The second-largest natural lake in North Yorkshire, covering 100 acres yet still only 800m long, it should be on every paddler's bucket list.

## The Lowdown

**DIFFICULTY** 💧

**WATER TYPE** Small lake

**DISTANCE** Variable (1.6km circumference)

**PARKING** Beach car park

**WHAT3WORDS** ///partly.widen.notice

**LAUNCH** Flat stone beach

## A brief history

Naturally formed at the end of the last Ice Age, this lake was created when sediment was left behind from the retreating glacier, damming the valley. Two large stones at the edge of the lake, locally known as the Mermaid Stones, are Shap granite boulders left by the melting ice. It has been pretty much left alone and undisturbed from any kind of commercial development ever since. When arriving at Semerwater, you almost

RIGHT Overlooking Semerwater.

OVERLEAF Semerwater from the launch beach.

feel like you have been transported back in time to an age when life was simple and calm. The name Semerwater was derived from the Old English words 'Sae' and 'Mear', meaning lake and water.

'Semerwater rise, Semerwater sink, and bury the town all save the house where they gave me meat and drink.' This is the spell cast in the local folklore legend where it is said a travelling angel, disguised as a beggar, visited the town looking for food and drink. Repeatedly turned away by the rich and prosperous, he eventually came to the last house in the town, up on the hill. Not much more than a hovel, it was home to an elderly couple who took pity on the beggar and shared the last of their bread and milk. The next evening, he cast the spell and almost immediately the town below was left flooded, sparing only their house and leaving the beautiful lake we have today.

## The paddle

Arriving at the car park you will see signage directing you to Low Blean Farm 300m up the road, where you can pay for parking and a small fee to access the water. This is a working farm so often unattended. If there is no one around, there is an honesty box attached to the gate.

The car park is an extension of the stony beach. The stones are quite flat, but I would still recommend footwear when entering the water. The beach slopes gently into the water so take care with fins if using a SUP. Once on the water, you are free to explore the whole of the lake – just be mindful of any anglers who could be using the easterly bankside. The lake is quite shallow at 1.2–1.8m deep, so can be an excellent place for beginners or those a little nervous of deeper waters. Starting on the lake near Semerwater Bridge, paddle beneath the towering Green Scar Mire Crag to the north and Blean High Pasture to the south. The lake's circumference is around 1.6km in length.

## Wildlife

There is a **nature reserve** to the south west end of the lake. In spring and summer you can spot a variety of birds including **curlews**, **oystercatchers**, **sand martins**, **lapwings** and **peregrine falcons**. **Ospreys** have recently been spotted nesting in nearby Wensleydale. **Roe deer**, **stoats** and **brown hare** are common sights around the lake.

## Food stops

• The nearby **Rose and Crown Hotel** in the village of Bainbridge is one of the oldest hotels in Yorkshire and serves food daily. They are famous for their giant filled Yorkshire puddings, an absolute must when visiting Yorkshire.
• **The Bake-Well** in Askrigg is open seven days a week serving coffee, teas and homemade hot and cold food to eat in or take away.

## Getting there

• **By car** – From the A684, turn on to Blean Lane 400m east of Bainbridge, signposted Semerwater. At the T-junction, turn right and follow the road to the lake on the left-hand side.

## NEED TO KNOW

■ Due to the remote nature of Semerwater, there are no toilet or changing facilities.
■ The gently sloping stone beach extends quite far into the water so always take care with your fin.

• **By train** – The nearest station is Garsdale, on the Settle to Carlisle line.
• **By bus** – The 156 Hawes to Leyburn bus stops in Bainbridge village, 4km from Semerwater.

## Other activities

The Yorkshire Dales are a haven for **cycling** enthusiasts both on and off road: the Buttertubs Pass, made famous by its inclusion in 2014's Tour de France, is less than 16km away. For mountain bikers, there is an abundance of trails. The Bainbridge to Semerwater loop is a 22.5km trail with 600m of ascent and is rated as an intermediate route. For hikers, the Yorkshire Three Peaks hiking route is within 32km.

# 19 ELLERTON LAKE

Surrounded by open countryside, Ellerton Lake has 60 acres of crystal-clear spring-fed freshwater. It is said to have the cleanest water for swimming in the North of England and on a calm day it's a common sight to see carp peacefully swimming underneath you.

## The Lowdown

**DIFFICULTY**

**WATER TYPE** Lake

**DISTANCE** Variable (1.5km circumference)

**PARKING** Ellerton Lake car park

**WHAT3WORDS** ///reach.dynamics.reduction

**LAUNCH** Beach

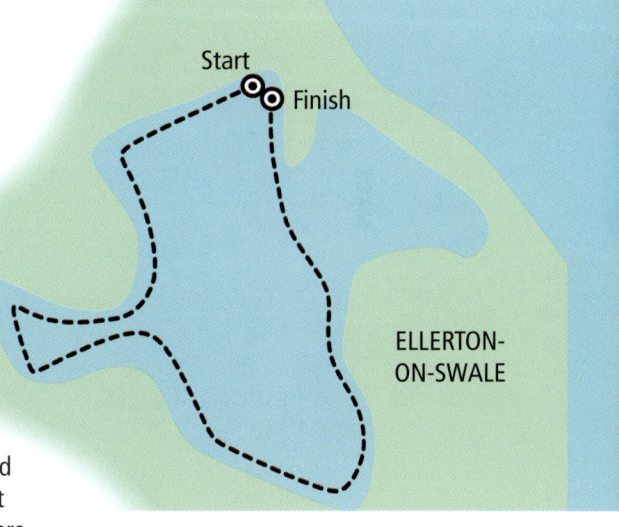

Start / Finish

ELLERTON-ON-SWALE

**A brief history** Ellerton Lake is located in the village of Ellerton-on-Swale, 1.6km east of Catterick, with a population of approximately 110. The village is entered in the Domesday Book, which states that it belonged to Count Alan and had six villagers. It's also the birthplace of Henry Jenkins, who died in 1670, apparently at the remarkable age of 169! A memorial obelisk is placed over his grave in the nearby churchyard. The lake, a former gravel quarry, is now a family-owned watersports centre, perfect for all non-motorised watersports.

LEFT River Bain into Semerwater.

RIGHT Danny playing SUP polo (credit SUP Active Yorkshire).

## The paddle

Access to the water is from the beach at the west side of the car park. Take a little care as you walk into the water as there are a few stones underfoot, but the water is soon deep enough to clear your fin. Once on the water, there is a small section of poles marking out a shallow part to be avoided. A full loop of the lake is 1.5km and, aside from the swimming area, you are free to paddle the whole lake. There is also a little slalom practice section in one corner that is worth trying. SUP Active Yorkshire are located on site and are available if you need to hire any equipment, as well as providing introductory SUP lessons, SUP yoga workshops and the SUPer fun activity of SUP polo. They also specialise in adaptive SUP sessions.

## Wildlife

The lake is well stocked with carp, pike and tench, and on calm days you can easily see the fish swimming below the surface.

## Food stops

Ellerton Lakeside Café and Green Frog Garden Shop in the village is open 9–5 Monday to Saturday. The café is renowned for quality food, sourcing all their products from within Yorkshire.

## NEED TO KNOW

■ There is a fee to access the water, payable at the entrance to the park.

■ There are toilets and changing facilities with showers on site.

■ Dogs are not permitted on site.

■ A PFD must be worn at all times on the water.

## Getting there

• **By car** – Leave the A1(M) at Brompton, following signs to Scorton. Stay on the B6271 where it turns right. After 1.6km, Ellerton Lake is found on the right.
• **By train** – The nearest stations are Darlington and Northallerton on the East Coast Main Line.
• **By bus** – There are limited bus routes to Ellerton, but Catterick can be reached from Darlington.

## Other activities

• With the lake's separate swimming area and plenty of quiet, undulating roads around Ellerton Lake, it is a popular location for triathletes and cyclists.

BELOW SUP Fit and social session (credit SUP Active Yorkshire).

## ANECDOTE FROM ELLERTON LAKE

*Apart from childhood holidays on the North East coast, I didn't grow up around water. My first taste of a watersport came at Ellerton Lake. I squeezed myself into a skin-tight wetsuit, slipped into the water and experienced my first ever open water swim. I was mesmerised by how crystal clear the water was. Before my visit, I had been told about the submerged cars, boats and even a caravan that divers use for training and exploration. It was quite a surreal moment when, swimming across the surface of the water, a large dark object glided along the lake-bed below me. It took a little while before I realised it wasn't a monster from the deep, but actually a diver heading to one of the submerged wrecks. I may have only been in the lake a short time, but it was long enough for me to appreciate how special water can be.*

*I spent many years swimming at Ellerton. The lake is divided into two sections, the swim area and the boating area, separated by a line of marker buoys. This helps keep the swimmers safe from any stray paddlers. Eventually, having progressed from swimming to paddling, I had a chance to explore the whole of the lake. On one occasion I was happily paddling around, minding my own business and lost in my own thoughts. The next thing I knew, I heard a loud bang coming from the front end of the board. My first thoughts are not repeatable in a family book, but suffice to say I thought that either I'd strayed into the swim area, or a stray swimmer had come into the main lake. This lasted for a couple of seconds before I realised I was actually nowhere near the swimmers and the culprit was more likely one of the many fish in the lake that thought the nose of my board was his next meal.*

• The lake has an array of **sunken boats, cars** and **caravans**, making it a great location for divers.
• There is a **caravan and motorhome site** adjacent to the lake, with private access to the water.

RIGHT Adaptive SUP session (credit SUP Active Yorkshire).

# 20 PRESTON PARK TO YARM

During summer, the warm, gentle, calm and still waters of the River Tees provide an excellent introduction for beginner paddlers to experience some longer river paddling. This meandering river treats paddlers to some stunning views of lush greenery and large gardens cascading down to the riverbank. It's a wonderful opportunity to escape the hustle and bustle of modern life and reconnect with nature.

## The Lowdown

**DIFFICULTY** 🌢🌢

**WATER TYPE**  River

**DISTANCE**  10km (round trip)

**PARKING**  Preston Park Museum and Grounds car park

**WHAT3WORDS**  ///forgives.monument.positives

**LAUNCH**  Jetty

## A brief history

The River Tees was at the heart of Teesside's industrial heritage. Shipbuilding on the river can be traced back to medieval times. By the 18th century, commercial shipbuilding was well established, boosted in the 19th century by the introduction of the Stockton & Darlington Railway. With the subsequent rise of the steel industry along its banks, the river soon became known as the 'Steel River'. Preston Park covers 100 acres and was developed into a public park after Preston Hall was bought by the Stockton Corporation in 1947; it was opened as a museum and park six years

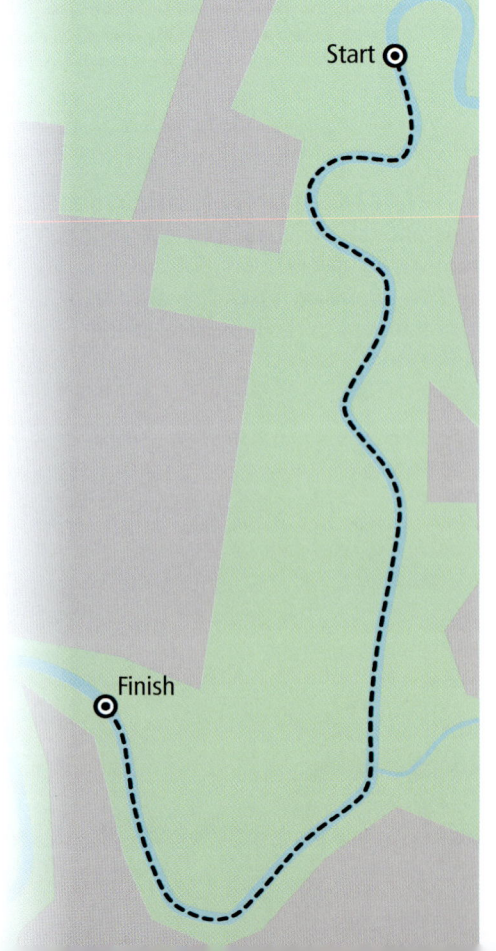

later. Until the Stockton Bridge opened in the late 18th century, the port of Yarm was the nearest point to the sea for crossing the River Tees. Stockton was also the birthplace of John Walker, who invented the friction match.

## The paddle
Parking is available in Preston Park Museum and Grounds; head towards the overflow car park as it's a little nearer the river. In summer you can park on the grass and it's only a short walk to the river's access jetty. If the field is closed off due to wet weather, follow the well-maintained path through the park.

Once on the water, head right along the open straight section of river; you may experience some breeze due to

ABOVE Early spring on the River Tees.

the prevailing wind but don't worry as it soon winds around and there is plenty of shelter from the riverbanks and trees that line the route. One kilometre into the paddle, you may catch glimpses through the trees of Eaglescliffe golf course on the right-hand side. One of the holes runs alongside the river, but the line of trees should provide enough protection against any stray shots! While paddling up the river it is easy to imagine you are deep in the English countryside, passing rolling hills and weeping willows. After 3km, you come to the little tributary River Leven on your left. It is very sheltered from any wind with overhanging trees but it is quite shallow in places. There can be the odd sunken branch and tree trunk too, so care is needed if you decide to explore along here. Continuing up the river, long, well-maintained gardens start to appear through the trees and soon Yarm School and boathouse are visible. From here, it's only another 500m before the spectacular 43-arch Yarm Viaduct and Yarm Bridge come into view.

Just before the bridge there is a large jetty. You can pull in here and exit the water for a spot of lunch before returning downstream to Preston Park.

## Wildlife
Although difficult to spot, the River Tees is home to populations of both great crested newts and otters. One of the best places to spot the otters is to take the little detour along the River Leven.

## Food stops
Yarm has an abundance of cafés, bars and restaurants.
• Finzi Artisan Pizza is just a short walk from the paddle get-out and sells individual pizza slices. I can't recommend highly enough the n'duja & ricotta – along with other Italian street food and pastries. It's the perfect interlude before heading back to Preston Park.

BELOW Passing under the bridges of Yarm.

## Getting there
• By car – Preston Park can be found south of Stockton, just off the A135 Yarm road. If using satnav, enter the postcode TS18 3RJ.
• By train – Eaglescliffe station, operated by Northern Rail, is about a 12-minute walk away.
• By bus – Arriva North East service No 7 stops just outside the park.

## Other activities
There are plenty of activities for all the family inside the park, including Butterfly World, a skate park and an adventure park. Step back in time and visit the Victorian Street inside the park's museum for a glimpse of what life was like in the 19th century.

## NEED TO KNOW

■ There are toilets and changing facilities available in the park.

■ This paddle heads upstream to Yarm. If you would like a shorter, easier paddle then it's possible to start at Yarm and paddle with the flow to Preston Park.

# 21 RUNSWICK BAY TO STAITHES

**The sandy beach at Runswick Bay is a true jewel in the crown of the North East.** The stunning views of the cliffs along the 'Dinosaur Coast' and the quaint, quirky fishing village of Staithes are also unforgettable seaside experiences. This charming stretch of coastline is definitely worth the trip.

## The Lowdown

**DIFFICULTY** ● ● ●

**WATER TYPE** Sea

**DISTANCE** 11km (round trip)

**PARKING** Car park

**WHAT3WORDS** ///haven.cello.news

**LAUNCH** Beach

## A brief history

This section of coastline is known as the 'Dinosaur Coast' due to the ancient fossils, many dating back to the Jurassic era, that have been discovered here. The fragile cliffs, rich in these fossils, are composed of layers of shale, sandstone and limestone, which have been gradually shaped by erosion over millions of years.

The village of Runswick Bay was almost completely demolished by a catastrophic landslide in 1682. Fortunately, no lives were lost, and the residents rebuilt the village a little further south, perched on the side of the cliffs.

The fishing village of Staithes dates back to the 16th century and, in my view, it is simply breathtaking. Once one of the largest fishing ports along the North Sea coast, it was known for its large fleet of fishing boats, known locally as 'cobles'. The renowned explorer Captain James Cook worked in the local grocer's here before moving to Whitby and beginning his naval career.

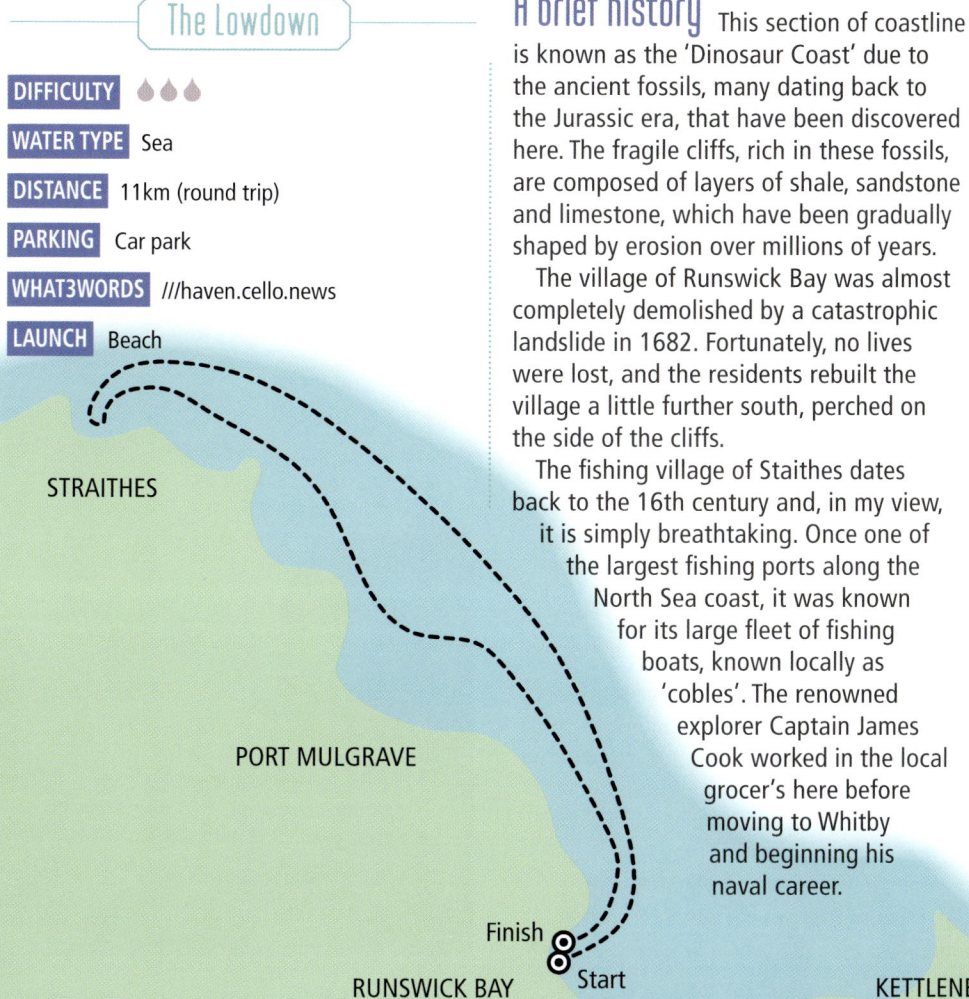

STRAITHES

PORT MULGRAVE

Finish

Start

RUNSWICK BAY

KETTLENESS

## The paddle

The road leading from the car park down to the beach is quite steep; follow it around to the right to reach the main beach. Runswick Bay was named Beach of the Year in the 2020 *Sunday Times* Beach Guide and was described as being 'close to perfection'. Nestled within the high cliffs, the bay's calm waters make it an ideal spot for beginners or those looking to gain sea paddling experience. Spanning over a kilometre, the bay offers plenty of space if you prefer to stay close to shore, enjoying a family beach day or fossil-hunting along the shoreline.

If you are looking to explore further, it's just over 5km to the beautiful fishing village of Staithes. From the bay, paddle out and bear left, following the coastline's cliffs. After about 2.5km you'll reach the harbour of Port Mulgrave. Built in 1856 to export ironstone to the shipyards at Jarrow, the port operated until 1920. It then fell into decline, and during the Second World War the Royal Engineers destroyed the harbour's breakwater as a defensive measure to help prevent German invasion.

There is a reef that hugs the base of the cliffs and stretches about 200m out to sea. If you're paddling close to shore, be mindful that the water can get a little bumpy, depending on conditions. As you approach Staithes harbour, it's worth taking a wide line behind any breaking waves over the reef. This not only makes for a smoother paddle but also rewards you with a fantastic

ABOVE Boats and kayaks lined up on the slipway.

RIGHT Sunrise over Runswick Bay.

BELOW Staithes in the distance nestled between the cliffs.

view of the little fishing village. Once inside the harbour, you can exit via the steps on the left-hand side.

It's well worth exploring this quaint village with its narrow, winding streets. One of these, Dog Loup, is only 46cm wide and is claimed to be the narrowest alley in the world. Parking within the village is limited, with the main car park at the top of the hill.

However, if you plan to paddle one way, it's possible to bring a car down to the harbour for a pick-up.

## Wildlife

**Cormorants** and **shags** can be spotted perched on the rocks or diving for fish. In spring and early summer, **puffins** can be seen flying low over the water. Keep an eye out for an inquisitive **seal** or a pod of **dolphins**.

## Food stops

• **Tides Coffee Bar and Beach Shop** is right on the seafront in Runswick Bay and serves hot and cold drinks, light snacks and the most delicious ice cream.
• **The Cod and Lobster** on Staithes seafront, overlooking the harbour, is a traditional pub serving cask ales, spirits and wines as well as traditional home-cooked meals. Their signature dish, Cod and Lobster, is amazing! It's a perfect stop for a mid-paddle meal.

## Getting there

• **By car** – From Runswick, follow the signs to Runswick Bay Beach – the road is very steep. There are two car parks: park in the public car park, the lower one is reserved for residents.
• **By train** – The nearest station is Whitby, 14km away.

• **By bus** – The X4 bus runs between Whitby and Middlesbrough, stopping at Runswick Bay.

## Other activities

• **The Cleveland Way** long-distance walking path passes right through Runswick Bay and Staithes.
• **Saltburn Cliff Tramway** is the oldest water-balanced funicular still in operation in Britain and links the Victorian town of Saltburn to the only surviving pleasure pier on the North East coast.

## NEED TO KNOW

■ There are several toilets in the village – follow the path behind Tides coffee shop.

■ The access to both Runswick Bay and Staithes is down very steep banks. It can be difficult for anyone with mobility issues.

■ Although the water inside the bay can be nice and calm, once you paddle out and along the coastline the conditions can change quickly. There are not many places to get out between the two villages.

# 22 WHITBY

'For a moment or two, I could see nothing, as the shadow of a cloud obscured St Mary's Church and all around it. Then as the cloud passed, I could see the ruins of the abbey coming into view, and as the edge of a narrow band of light as sharp as a sword-cut moved along, the church and churchyard became gradually visible... it seemed to me as though something dark stood behind the seat where the white figure shone, and bent over it. I could not tell what it was, whether man or beast, I could not tell' – Bram Stoker, *Dracula*.

## The Lowdown

**DIFFICULTY**

**WATER TYPE** River

**DISTANCE** 4.5km (round trip)

**PARKING** Car park

**WHAT3WORDS** ///feared.young.covenants

**LAUNCH** Slipway

## A brief history

Whitby is steeped in history and maritime heritage. The town of Whitby was founded in the 7th century with the establishment of Whitby Abbey by St Hilda in AD 657. During the Synod of Whitby in AD 664, the dates of Easter were agreed and the Roman and Celtic Christian traditions were united, with Roman Christianity predominating in England until Henry VIII's infamous break with Rome. Fast-forward to 1897, and the abbey's dramatic scenery and Gothic architecture were the inspiration behind Bram Stoker's novel *Dracula*.

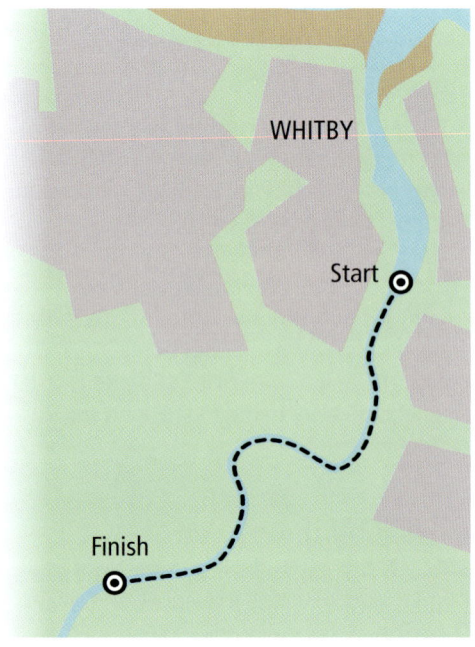

RIGHT The harbour and abbey.

During the 18th century, Whitby gained fame as a shipbuilding hub. Notably, James Cook began his illustrious seafaring career in the town, launching HMS *Endeavour* on his first voyage of discovery to Australia. Today, the *Bark Endeavour Whitby*, a life-size replica of HMS *Endeavour*, is moored in the harbour and serves as an interactive museum, café and bar.

## The paddle

Launch from the slipway at the southernmost part of the car park. Remember that this is a working harbour so be mindful of any marine activity. Once on the water, take a minute to view the majestic sight of Whitby Abbey up on the hill overlooking the harbour. Keep to the right side as you head upriver away from the harbour towards Ruswarp. The River Esk can be quite shallow. Although you should keep to the right, be careful not to get too close to the edge once you pass under the A171 road bridge, particularly if you have a fin, as there is a chance you could catch the bottom.

Paddling up the mirror-glass water, you soon reach the Grade II listed Larpool Viaduct. Opened in 1885 for the Scarborough and Whitby Railway, the viaduct's proximity to the sea necessitated a construction method that avoided the use of iron to prevent corrosion. Instead, it was built with brick and cement, featuring 13 arches and spanning 279m, with a height of 37m. The bridge closed to trains in 1965 and is now part of the Scarborough to Whitby Rail Trail cycle route.

Once past the viaduct, you may see a steam train passing by on the right-hand side if you are lucky, and then the impressive spire of St Bartholomew's Church comes into view through the trees. As you round the bend, you reach the village of Ruswarp. Stop on the island for a drink or a picnic before returning to Whitby.

## Wildlife

• The River Esk is home to Yorkshire's only population of **freshwater pearl mussels.** There are several ongoing projects along the river that aim to protect this endangered species. This is also a good reminder always to wash your paddle craft to help

prevent the spread of signal crayfish and other invasive species that can decimate riverbeds.

• There are regular sightings of a large **bull seal** that has made the area west of the viaduct its home.

• **Herons** and **egrets** are common along this section of river.

## Food stops

Whitby has an abundance of cafés, bars, restaurants and chippies. **Trenchers Restaurant & Takeaway** is an award-winning fish and chip restaurant that sits on Whitby's harbour-side. **The Magpie Café** on Pier Road is one of the most popular fish restaurants in town.

## Getting there

• **By car** – From the A174, take the Bagdale road towards Whitby town centre and the river. Turn right on to Langborne Road at the mini roundabout and follow this to the car park on the left. Park at the far end, near the access slipway.

• **By train** – Whitby is on the Esk Valley line from Middlesbrough. The car park is a 6-minute walk from the station.

• **By bus** – The nearest bus stop is outside the Co-op on Langhorne Rd, a 4-minute walk away. Whitby's main bus station is opposite the train station.

## Other activities

• **Whitby Walk with Heritage Trail** is a self-guided walking trail taking in nine sculptures, created by local sculptor Emma Stothard, depicting some of the town's most famous characters.

• **Climb the infamous 199 steps** that lead up to Whitby Abbey and immerse yourself in the haunting beauty of this ancient site.

• **Take a trip on the *Bark Endeavour***, sing sea shanties and learn all about Captain Cook's life. Look out for the crocodile shaped cliff face and a rocky whale – these are just some of the highlights of this short boat trip along the Whitby coastline.

## NEED TO KNOW

■ There are toilets in the car park.

■ Take care when accessing and exiting the water, particularly around the harbour.

■ This section of the River Esk is tidal and can get quite shallow at low to mid tides.

BELOW Larpool Viaduct.

# 23 RIPON CANAL TO BOROUGHBRIDGE

At 3.7km long, Ripon Canal may be one of the shortest canals in Yorkshire, but it is certainly one of the prettiest. The paddle starts in the heart of the medieval city of Ripon – steeped in history, it's the oldest city in England and, with a population of under 17,000, it's also the third smallest city. It is fair to say that everything about Ripon and its canal is small but perfectly formed.

## The Lowdown

**DIFFICULTY** ● to ●●●

**WATER TYPE** Canal

**DISTANCE** 5km **Rhodesfield Lock to Oxclose Lock** (round trip)
10.5km **Rhodesfield Lock to Boroughbridge** (one way)

**PARKING** Car park

**WHAT3WORDS** ///senders.levels.trainer

**LAUNCH** Jetty

RIPON

Start

Lock

Lock

WEIR (keep left)

Lock

Finish

BOROUGHBRIDGE

## A brief history

The canal was built by canal engineer William Jessop and opened in 1773 to link the city of Ripon with the River Ure. It makes up the northern length of the Ure Navigation. The River Ure joins the River Swale to form the Yorkshire Ouse Navigation. Coal was the main cargo carried into the city from the Yorkshire coalfields, with lead and agricultural produce going the other way. It fell into disrepair in the early 1900s, due to competition from the railways bringing in coal from Durham, and was officially abandoned in the 1950s. The Ripon Motor Boat Club was instrumental in pushing forward the restoration of the canal, which began in 1961. The first half reopened in the mid-80s and the restoration was finally fully completed in 1996.

## The paddle

**Part 1 Rhodesfield Lock to Oxclose Lock return (5km)**

From the car park at Rhodesfield Lock, head through the gate to the canal. Turning left, go beyond the lock and follow the towpath down to the jetty. Once on the water, you can see the Bell Furrows Lock a few hundred metres ahead of you – this is the first portage of the paddle. Once you reach the lock gates, exit at the left-hand side jetty and it's only a short walk around to get to the next section. Take a few steps down. There is a little drop to the water, so take a bit of care when getting back on your craft.

You are now treated to an uninterrupted tranquil paddle, passing through the red-brick arches of the Nicholson Bridge

and Renton's Bridge before reaching the turnaround point at Oxclose Lock. If you are looking for a longer paddle, it's possible to portage here and join the River Ouse down to Boroughbridge. This adds another 8km to the length of the paddle. Check the water level indicator board on the low side of the lock wall before proceeding as this gives a good guide to the strength of the river flow for the upstream paddle back.

There are plenty of moorings along both sides of the canal and it's always worth stopping south of the Nicholson Bridge, where there is a bird hide overlooking the Ripon City Wetlands and the racecourse, before arriving back at the car park.

**Part 2 Rhodesfield Lock to Boroughbridge one way (10.5km)**
After the lock, you are now paddling with the gentle flow of the river. After around 1.5km you pass Newby Hall and its miniature steam railway. After another kilometre, you come to a fork in the river. There is a large sign directing all traffic to turn right – this brings you to Westwick Lock and avoids the weir. A short portage takes you back to the river, where you are treated to 5km of tranquil tree-lined paddling down to Boroughbridge. One kilometre after passing under the A1 bridge, you will see a large orange barrier. Keep to the left and 200m further down you can get out under the bridge. The car park is on the right-hand side.

## Wildlife
Ripon City Wetlands lie adjacent to the canal, spanning 41ha. The wetlands are a year-round haven for wildlife – keep an eye out for avocets, little ringed plovers, kingfishers and otters among the reed beds. If you're on the water during autumn, it's the perfect place to see the amazing spectacle of starling murmurations.

## Food stops
Ripon town centre is less than 1.5km away with an abundance of cafés, restaurants, pubs and Yorkshire tearooms. The Anchor Inn next to the car park at Boroughbridge is a dog-friendly traditional pub.

## Getting there
• By car – From the A61, take the B6265 (Boroughbridge Road) and the car park is 500m on the right.
• By train – The nearest stations are Harrogate and Leeds, both 18km from Ripon.
• By bus – The No 822 bus serves Ripon. The nearest bus stop is Skelldale Caravan Park on Boroughbridge Road, a 2-minute walk from the launch point.

## Other activities
The towpath runs alongside the canal, perfect for anyone wanting to stay close to the paddlers without being on the water. While in the area, it's worthwhile visiting Newby Hall, Fountains Abbey and the 12th-century Ripon Cathedral. A 10-minute drive from Ripon takes you to Lightwater Valley Family Adventure Park.

## NEED TO KNOW

■ A waterways licence is needed to paddle the canal. This can be obtained from the Paddle UK website: paddleuk.org.uk.

■ If you are intending to continue on to Boroughbridge, check the coloured strip on the lower side of Oxclose Lock. If you can see green then you are good to go.

LEFT Ripon Canal (credit SUP Active Yorkshire).

ABOVE Low-lying mist on the water.          BELOW Knaresborough Bridge (credit SUP Active Yorkshire).

# 24 YORK – RIVER OUSE

**Paddling through the medieval city of York,** the tranquil waters of the Ouse allow you to soak in York's rich history and unique scenery, including the majestic York Minster and the ancient city walls. Paddling under its historic bridges is a perfect way to explore one of England's most storied cities.

## The Lowdown

**DIFFICULTY** 💧 to 💧💧

**WATER TYPE** River

**DISTANCE** Up to 12km (round trip)

**PARKING** Rowntree Park car park

**WHAT3WORDS** ///circle.bounty.shares

**LAUNCH** Jetty

## A brief history

York was founded by the Romans in AD 71 as Eboracum. The city became a significant military base and, later, an imperial seat where Constantine the Great was proclaimed emperor. After the Romans, the city fell under Anglo-Saxon control and was renamed Eoforwic. In AD 866 the Vikings captured York, transforming it into Jorvik, a bustling hub of trade and culture. The Vikings left a lasting imprint, evident in the city's layout and archaeology.

Following the Norman Conquest in 1066, York flourished as a medieval stronghold. The construction of York Minster, one of the largest Gothic cathedrals in Northern Europe, began in the 13th century.

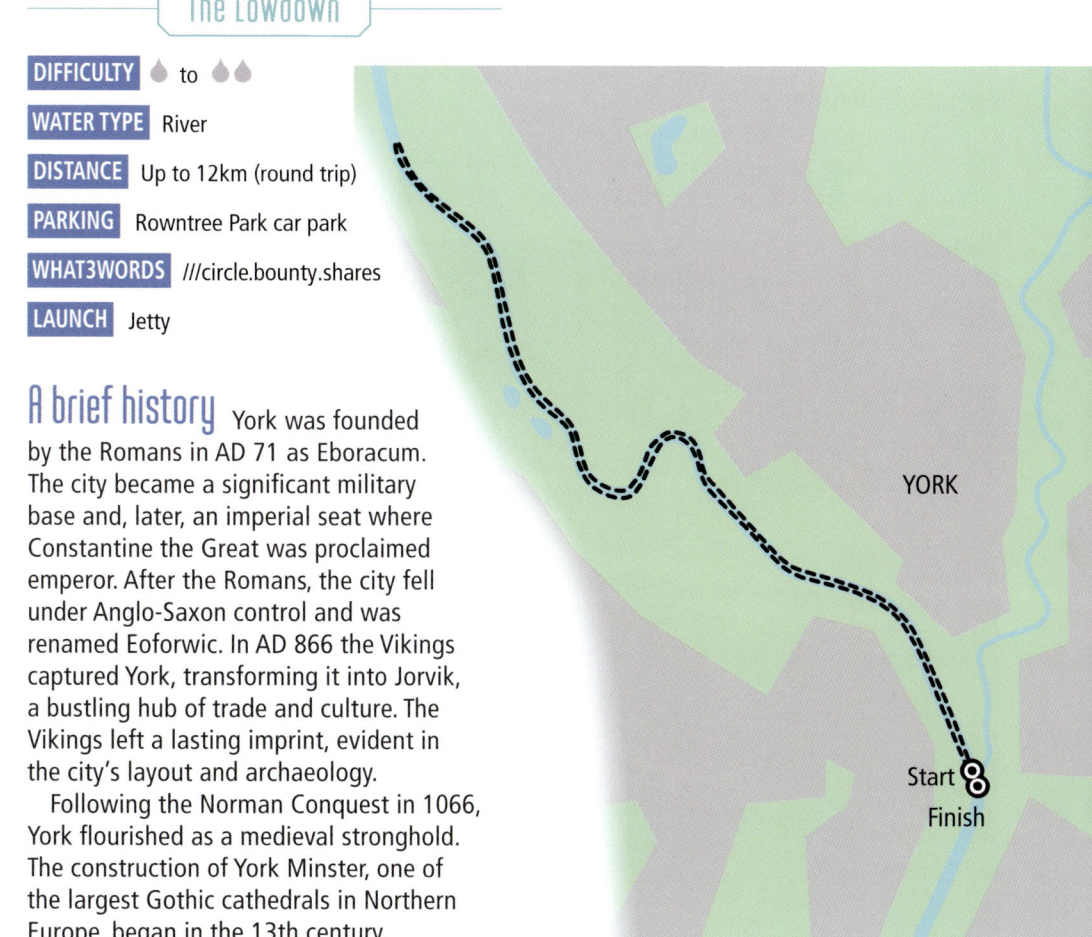

Throughout the medieval period, the city grew as a centre of commerce and religion. Today, York retains its historical charm, with its well-preserved city walls, medieval streets like the Shambles, and significant archaeological sites like Clifford's Tower. It's a vibrant city, blending its rich heritage with contemporary culture.

## The paddle

From the Rowntree Park car park, turn left and it's a short 60m walk to the steps leading down to the water. Once on the water, make your way over to the opposite side and head north – you can see the bridges of the city in the distance. Paddling up the river, it's clear to see the rich industrial heritage, notably the impressive Waterfront House, once a bonded warehouse and now a luxury apartment complex. The first bridge you pass under is the Gothic-style Skeldergate Bridge, built in 1878 to help ease congestion on the ferry crossing. It's worth stopping to admire the ornate ironwork six-pointed stars and the famous white rose of York, repeated across the span of the parapet.

You are now in the heart of the city. To the left is Woodsmill Quay, once a large flour mill and now converted into shops, offices and apartments. To the right is the Kings Arms pub; built in the early 17th century, it's the only surviving building from what was once First Water Lane, a medieval street demolished in 1852 during a slum clearance programme.

Next up is the Ouse Bridge. There have been many incarnations of this bridge. Originally, the Vikings built a wooden bridge; unfortunately, it collapsed under the weight of a crowd gathering to greet St William of York on his return from exile. In the 12th century it was replaced with a stone bridge, and in 1367 the earliest

RIGHT River Ouse.

BELOW Tom heading towards Ouse Bridge.

recorded public toilets in Yorkshire – and, most likely, in England – were opened on the bridge. It was rebuilt in 1821 as the bridge you see today.

You are now coming to Lendal Bridge, a cast-iron single-span bridge designed by Thomas Page, who also designed London's Westminster Bridge. Lendal Bridge stands on the site of a former rope-ferry between the city walls. It connects two medieval towers, Lendal Tower on the right bank and Barker Tower on the left.

After Lendal Bridge, the landscape is more serene and parklike. To the right is York Museum Gardens, 10 acres of botanical gardens set around York Museum and the ruins of St Mary's Abbey.

Up ahead you are approaching the Scarborough railway bridge. Scarborough Bridge was originally built in 1845 to carry the rail line between York and Scarborough.

It has been altered and improved over the years, with a wide pedestrian path on the south side creating a car-free route from the station to the city centre. The National Railway Museum is on the left bank just after the bridge and houses the iconic steam locomotive the *Flying Scotsman*.

You are now leaving behind the city and are treated to 4km of meandering river with pleasant green fields and tree-lined paddling, passing under the Clifton Bridge. There are a few beaches along the route if you want to stop for a rest or picnic before reaching the turnaround point at the main York Bypass Bridge. The return to York will come quickly as you are now paddling with the flow of the river. If you're lucky, you will see Two Hoots Ice Cream Boat along the river. I can recommend stopping and enjoying an ice cream before returning to the car park.

## Wildlife
Look out for kingfishers, swans and geese, and if you're lucky you can spot otters in the banksides north of the city.

## Food stops
Rowntree Park Reading Café in Rowntree Park serves breakfast and seasonal home-cooked food all day.

## Getting there
• By car – From the A19, follow signs for Rowntree Park. The car park is on Terry Avenue, on the right-hand side.
• By train – York is on the East Coast Main line and trains run regularly from London's King's Cross.
• By bus – The nearest bus stop is Bishopthorpe Road Shops, a 2-minute ride from York railway station.

## Other activities
It's impossible to include enough history in this book and it is well worth taking a self-guided walking tour of this fabulous city. Tours can be purchased from www.viator.com and downloaded to a smartphone. Must-see places include the National Railway Museum, York Minster and the Shambles. Rowntree Park has plenty of open space and a large children's play area.

## NEED TO KNOW
■ There are toilets in Rowntree Park, adjacent to the car park.

■ A waterways licence is needed to paddle on the river. This can be obtained from the Paddle UK website: paddleuk.org.uk.

■ The river can get quite busy with traffic, particularly during summer, so always paddle on the right-hand side.

■ The river is prone to flooding and can rise 5m above normal levels so always check forecasts and river levels before undertaking this paddle. Details can be found on the government website: check-for-flooding.service. gov.uk/station/8208.

BELOW Redundant cranes at Woodsmill Quay.

# 25 RIVER DERWENT – KIRKHAM PRIORY TO STAMFORD BRIDGE

Starting at Kirkham Priory and ending in the village of Stamford Bridge, the River Derwent offers a paddling adventure like no other. Navigate fallen trees, Archimedes screws, and trek through the woods to bypass weirs. This is a paddle sport trip to remember.

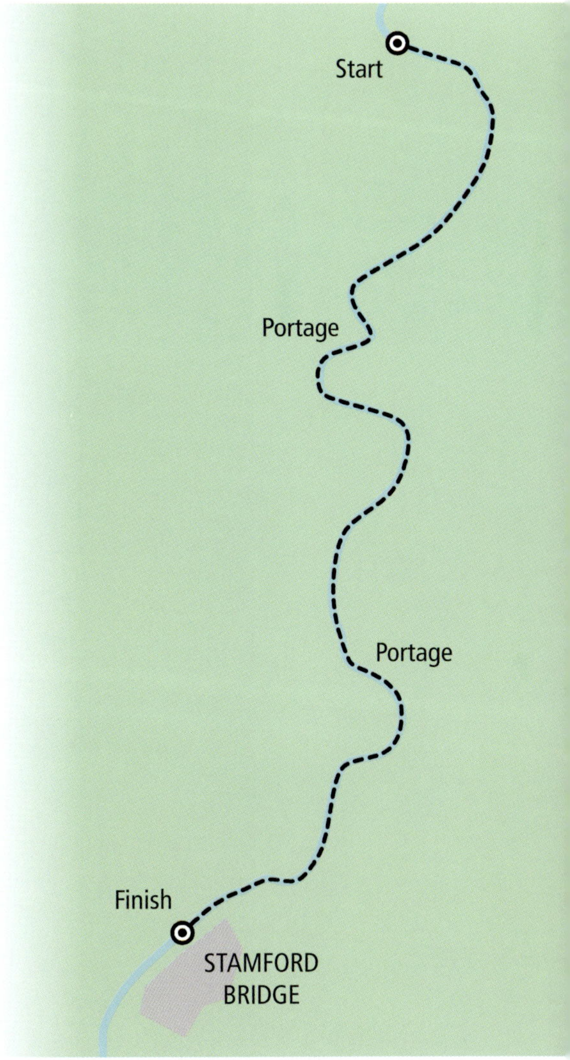

## The Lowdown

**DIFFICULTY** ▲▲▲

**WATER TYPE**  River

**DISTANCE**  17km (one way)

**PARKING**  Kirkham Priory car park

**WHAT3WORDS**  ///butlers.revisits.dribble

**LAUNCH**  Riverside

## A brief history

According to legend, Walter I'Espec, Lord of Helmsley, built Kirkham Priory in the 1120s in memory of his son, who was tragically killed in a horse-riding accident. During the Second World War, the priory was visited by Winston Churchill and became a secret testing area for the D-Day landing vehicles.

Stamford Bridge played host to a pivotal battle in 1066. King Harold defeated the Norwegians, which ended the age of the Viking invasions. Unfortunately, less than three weeks later a depleted army headed south to fight in the Battle of Hastings. It didn't end well for them.

OVERLEAF Kirkham Bridge.

# The paddle

### Section 1 Kirkham Priory to Howsham Mill (4km)

After parking in the priory car park, you will need to walk over the bridge and through the small gate that leads down to the river. Don't be tempted to access the water here as 150m further along is a weir. Instead, follow the path through a second gate and make your way through the trees to the water's edge. The water here is quite fast-moving, so take care when launching.

The river is relatively narrow and tranquil, winding through lush green countryside and overhanging trees. The trees not only appear from the sides and above but also from below, giving this section a real feel of adventure. At 4km, you can hear the water running at Howsham Mill. Originally an 18th-century watermill, it's now an environmental education centre. It also serves as a great place for a break and to explore. During the mill's restoration, an Archimedes screw turbine was installed to harness the river's flow to generate hydroelectricity. The easiest way to get off the water is from a small inlet on the left-hand side of the river. Follow the path to Howsham Mill.

### Section 2 Howsham to Buttercrambe (7km)

Access back to the water is down a small path to the left-hand side of the bridge wall, behind the building. The water rushes under the bridge and can look intimidating but it's not deep and if you keep to the side, you will avoid a little swim. Once back on the main river, the journey down to Buttercrambe is relatively gentle, and carries on the theme of adventure and undisturbed peace and tranquillity. At 11km you need to keep an eye out for the next weir. This one can creep up on you, but approximately 200m before you will see a large black cable crossing above the river. After this, exit the water from one of the small jetties on the left-hand side of the river.

### Section 3 Buttercrambe to Stamford Bridge (6km)

Walking from the field, cross the road and go through a five-bar gate leading to a path passing a small outbuilding to a jetty below the weir. The path may be overgrown, depending on the time of year, so watch out for the steps leading down towards the jetty.

The river starts to widen out a little on this last section; however, you are still quite secluded and sheltered as the river meanders through the rural landscape before arriving at Stamford Bridge. After approximately 16km, you'll see a caravan park. Take the right-hand channel, leaving the main river. Pass the caravan site and continue past another caravan site on the right. After an additional 100m, you'll find a stone landing jetty on the right-hand side.

## Wildlife Mallard ducks, mute swans

and the elusive kingfisher can be seen along the river. If you're lucky, you may spot a water vole along the riverbanks or roe deer among the trees.

## Food stops

• The Three Cups in Stamford Bridge is a country pub serving traditional pub classics and seasonal dishes.
• The Square Bakehouse in Stamford Bridge is an artisan bakery, perfect for stocking up on pastries and sweet treats.
• The Stone Trough Inn, Kirkham Abbey, is another traditional country pub, with an open fire.

## Getting there

• By car – From York, take the A66 towards Malton. At Whitwell, turn right onto Onhams Lane. Follow for 1.6km and the car park is on the right, just over Kirkham Bridge.
• By train – The nearest station is Malton,

ABOVE Howsham Mill.

on the York to Scarborough line.
• **By bus** – The nearest bus stop is Kirkham Abbey. Take the Ryedale Community Transport 184 from Malton.

## Other activities

Explore the riverside ruins of **Kirkham Priory**, a serene, atmospheric site maintained by English Heritage. Take a guided tour that delves into the priory's rich history, or simply relax with a picnic in the gardens.

   **Ellers Farm Distillery** – just outside Stamford Bridge, this eco-minded distillery turns Yorkshire apples into award-winning Dutch Barn Vodka. Take a tour, sample a few tipples, and hear the story behind their sustainable spirits.

## NEED TO KNOW

■ There are toilet facilities at both the start and end of the paddle.

■ This can be a demanding paddle, with long sections with little vehicle access. There are also several technical parts so it's best to paddle with a guide or group that is familiar with this route. SUP Yorkshire are very experienced paddlers and run regular paddle expeditions on the river (check out SUP Yorkshire's Facebook page for more details).

■ There are 11 tributaries that flow into the River Derwent. This can cause the river to flash-flood after heavy rain, so always check local river forecasts.

# 26 FLAMBOROUGH HEAD AND CAVES

Rising 122m from the sea below, the dramatic white chalk cliffs of Flamborough Head – with its coves, caves, arches and stacks – are a haven for wildlife and home to thousands of nesting seabirds. Paddling along this stunning coastline offers the chance to see puffins, kittiwakes and seals up close, while weaving through hidden caves and rocky outcrops. It makes for an unforgettable coastal adventure.

## The Lowdown

**DIFFICULTY** 🌢🌢🌢

**WATER TYPE** Sea

**DISTANCE** Up to 14km (round trip)

**PARKING** Car park

**WHAT3WORDS** ///allowable.enable.brand

**LAUNCH** Beach

**A brief history** Flamborough Head is one of the most spectacular areas of chalk cliffs in Britain. The chalk was formed during the Cretaceous period, when warm shallow seas rich in coral, phytoplankton and tiny marine organisms covered the area. Over millions of years, the remains of these creatures settled on the seabed, compacting into layers of chalk. Tectonic movements then forced these cliffs up out of the ocean.

There are two lighthouses on the headland. The older one was built in 1669 and is one of the oldest remaining complete lighthouses in England, although it was never actually lit. The new one, designed by Samuel Wyatt, was built in 1806 and was the first to use a powerful, revolving catoptric lens system, making it a landmark for advancing lighthouse technology.

RIGHT The view from one of the many caves along the cliffs (credit Shane Linford).

## The paddle

From the car park overlooking the bay, follow the path from the north-east end down to the beach. While it's true that this path is quite steep, the reward of the paddle certainly is worth the climb back up afterwards. There is so much to explore along this stunning coastline that it's almost impossible to pick a single route. You could spend hours just discovering caves and caverns, and if you paddle out and bear right, the breathtaking views of the chalk cliffs are truly incredible!

Whether you're paddling at low or high tide, the coastal vistas are amazing, though I find the two-hour window either side of high tide offers the best opportunities to explore the caves. One of the first landmarks you will notice is a rock formation known as the Drinking Dinosaur. From there you are treated to a series of mini adventures, each as captivating as the last. On a sunny day, the kaleidoscope of colours that fill the caves is a sight to behold.

If you wish to explore the coastline further, it is 7km from the start at North Landing round Flamborough Head to South Landing. This can be a challenging yet

LEFT Launching at North Landing Beach.

BELOW Paddling through the caves (credit Shane Linford).

rewarding section, with several coves and beaches. If you stop at any one of the many beaches, just be mindful: the chalk cliffs are prone to falling rocks from above. As you approach the apex of Flamborough Head, you can see the lighthouse on the cliffs above. Constructed by local builder John Matson without the aid of scaffolding, the lighthouse is still in use today to help mark the headland for passing ships heading into Bridlington and Scarborough. Don't be surprised if you hear a little snort from behind – it might be one or even several Atlantic grey seals escorting you past the Drinking Dinosaur, where they've made their home. If the tide is low, you may spot them basking on the rocks, so please be respectful and keep a good distance away. It is better to pass at high tide, avoiding the

ABOVE The Elephant (credit Shane Linford).

RIGHT Admiring the cliffs.

beaches and taking care not to startle them as you glide by. After rounding the point, it's another 3km to arrive at South Landing. There is a lifeboat station there with a small parking area where you could get picked up if you wanted to paddle this route one way.

## Wildlife
• **Harbour porpoises** are sometimes spotted in the area.
• During the summer, the cliffs echo with a cacophony of noise from the thousands of **breeding auks**, **gannets**, **gulls** and **puffins**.

## Food stops

• **The Caravel Bar** adjacent to the car park is open from mid-March until the end of October. It serves traditional pub grub, ice creams, teas and coffees.
• **The Headlands Family Restaurant and Cafe Bar** is right next to the old lighthouse. It is a family-run restaurant serving a wide variety of homemade hot and cold food, drinks and snacks.
• **The Seabirds Inn**, located in Flamborough, prides itself on serving great locally sourced food. Their menu changes regularly with the seasons to ensure the freshest ingredients.

## Getting there

• **By car** – From Flamborough, North Marine Road takes you all the way to North Landing car park.
• **By train** – The nearest station is Bridlington, on the Yorkshire Coast Line.

## NEED TO KNOW

■ Toilets are available at North Landing car park.

■ It's advisable to do this paddle only on calm days with no waves or swell.

■ Care is needed accessing the beach as the path is very steep.

• **By bus** – The 14 bus from Bridlington stops at Flamborough North Landing.

## Other activities

**The King Charles III England Coast Path** runs the length of the headland, providing great views of the coastline and opportunities to spot the wildlife.

# 27 SALTAIRE BREWERY TO BINGLEY FIVE RISE LOCKS

At nearly 210km long, the Leeds & Liverpool Canal offers countless places to explore. Paddling over a Grade II listed aqueduct, through ancient woodlands and past a UNESCO World Heritage Site, this section of the canal promises a truly unforgettable experience.

## The Lowdown

**DIFFICULTY** 💧💧

**WATER TYPE** Canal

**DISTANCE** 12km (one way)

**PARKING** Side of road

**WHAT3WORDS** ///value.diner.branded

**LAUNCH** Canal-side

## A brief history

The village of Saltaire derives its name from the surname of its founder, Sir Titus Salt, and the River Aire, which flows alongside. Born in 1803, Salt was a textile manufacturer, politician and philanthropist who envisioned a better way of living and working for his employees.

By 1850, Titus Salt was the largest employer in Bradford, and sought to consolidate his textile manufacturing operations into a single, more efficient location. Salts Mill opened in 1853. Its location beside the River Aire, the Leeds & Liverpool Canal and the Midland Railway provided excellent transport links for distributing goods.

Salt didn't stop with the mill; he went on to create the adjoining village of Saltaire, a purpose-built community, including housing, almshouses, shops, schools,

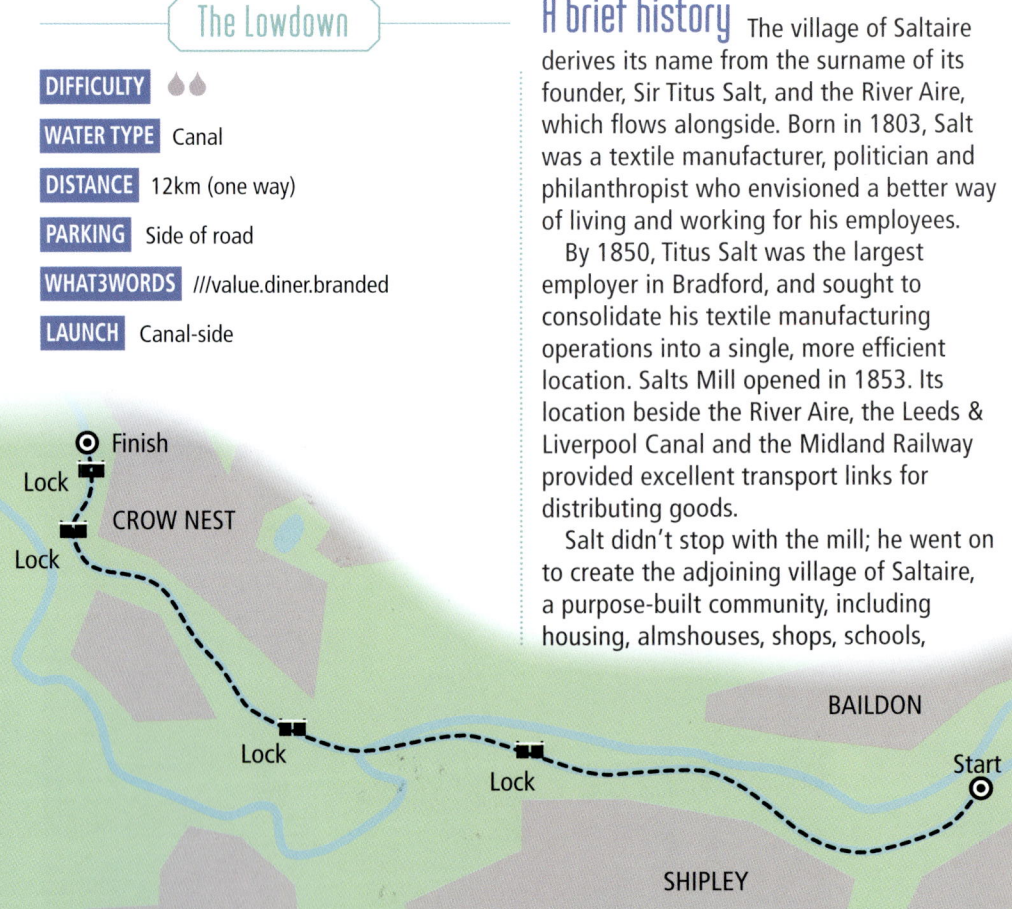

ABOVE Salts Mill.

an infirmary, a church, parks and leisure facilities. His vision was rooted in the belief that providing a clean, healthy environment for his workers would result in stronger, fitter and healthier employees, ultimately boosting productivity.

## The paddle

Launch opposite the Saltaire Brewery Taproom and head right. Just 200m in, you will encounter the first challenge of the day: Dock Swing Bridge. This bridge is very low and, depending on the water level, you may need to crouch or lie flat to pass beneath. Alternatively, you can exit the water to the right and portage around.

Next, you'll come to the quaint stone arch of Junction Bridge, which marks the junction with the Bradford Canal branch and allowed the tow horses to cross between the canals. You are now heading into the UNESCO World Heritage Site of Saltaire, and the jaw-dropping sight of Salts Mill. After 2.5km you reach Hirst Lock (No 19). Exit the water to the right-hand side and you have a 100m portage.

Re-enter the water after the bridge. Leaving urban Saltaire behind as you paddle

RIGHT Bingley Five Rise Locks (credit Shane Linford).

FAR RIGHT Reflections of the trees in the glass-calm waters along the canal.

through the ancient woodland of Hirst Wood, you soon arrive at the Seven Arches Aqueduct. Built in 1842, this elegant stone structure spans the River Aire with seven 10m-wide arches. Over time, the piers have shifted due to ground settlement, creating a noticeable lean when viewed from a distance. While the aqueduct remains structurally sound, this subtle tilt adds to its charm. After crossing the aqueduct, you pass under the bridge and arrive at Dowley Gap Locks (No 20 and 21), a pair of locks that rise in height 5m over a distance of 100m. Exit to the left-hand side.

Once back on the water, pass under the arch of bridge 205 and immediately on the left is The Fisherman's Inn. This is a great spot to stop for a drink or a bite to eat in their canal-side beer garden. Continuing along the canal, you will soon reach the market town of Bingley. As you paddle past the towering chimneys from the town's industrial past, you'll arrive at Bingley Three Rise Locks (No 22–24). Exit the water to the left-hand side to portage around this impressive staircase lock system, which rises 9m over a distance of 100m. After the Three Rise Locks, it's a short paddle to the magnificent Grade I listed Bingley Five Rise Locks. Standing twice the height of the Three Rise, this is the steepest flight of locks in the UK and rises 18.03m over just 100m, with a gradient of about 1:5. The intermediate and bottom gates are the tallest in the country.

At the top of the locks, you'll find the dog-friendly Five Rise Locks Cafe, a perfect place to rest and enjoy a treat after the climb. You can end your paddle here, continue further along the canal, or return to Saltaire for a well-deserved drink at the Brewery Taproom.

## Wildlife

Kingfishers are a common sight along the canal, and you'll often spot grey squirrels darting among the trees. Keep a keen eye out near Hirst Wood, and you might even catch a glimpse of an elusive otter.

## Food stops

• **Five Rise Locks Cafe** is a dog-friendly café serving a wide variety of hot and cold food and drinks.
• **The Fisherman's Inn** is located on the banks of the canal approaching Bingley, serving traditional pub classics.

## Getting there

• **By car** – Saltaire Brewery Taproom is located on Dockfield Road, Shipley.
• **By train** – The nearest station is Saltaire, a 10-minute walk to the launch spot.
• **By bus** – The nearest bus stop is adjacent to the train station.

## Other activities

• **The canal towpath** is perfect for walking and cycling.
• **The Shipley Glen Tramway**, one of the world's oldest funicular tramways, connects the elevated village of Baildon to Saltaire below, descending a steep 1:7 gradient.

## NEED TO KNOW

■ A waterways licence is needed to paddle the canal. This can be obtained from the Paddle UK website: paddleuk.org.uk.

■ There are no toilet or changing facilities at the start, but toilets are available if using the Taproom.

■ There are several portages along this route. The Dowley Gap Locks can be a little over a metre drop down to the water.

# 28 LEEDS WOODLESFORD CIRCULAR

The Woodlesford circular is a delightful mixed waterway route, starting on the still waters of the Aire & Calder Navigation and finishing with an exhilarating return paddle down the River Aire. The combination of tranquil canal and lively river creates a varied and enjoyable loop. If tranquil is more your type of paddling, then stay on the canal for a leisurely trip into the bustling and vibrant city of Leeds.

## The Lowdown

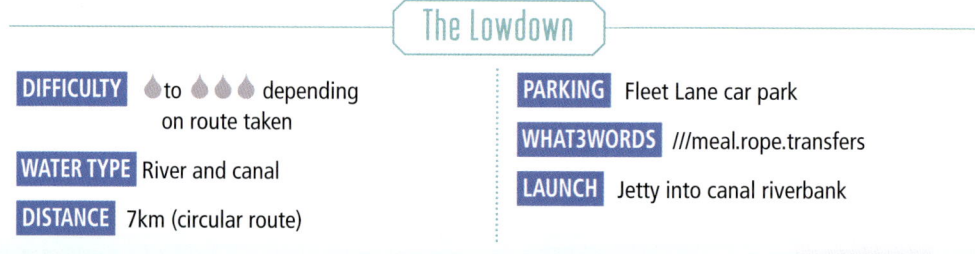

**DIFFICULTY** 🌢 to 🌢🌢🌢 depending on route taken

**WATER TYPE** River and canal

**DISTANCE** 7km (circular route)

**PARKING** Fleet Lane car park

**WHAT3WORDS** ///meal.rope.transfers

**LAUNCH** Jetty into canal riverbank

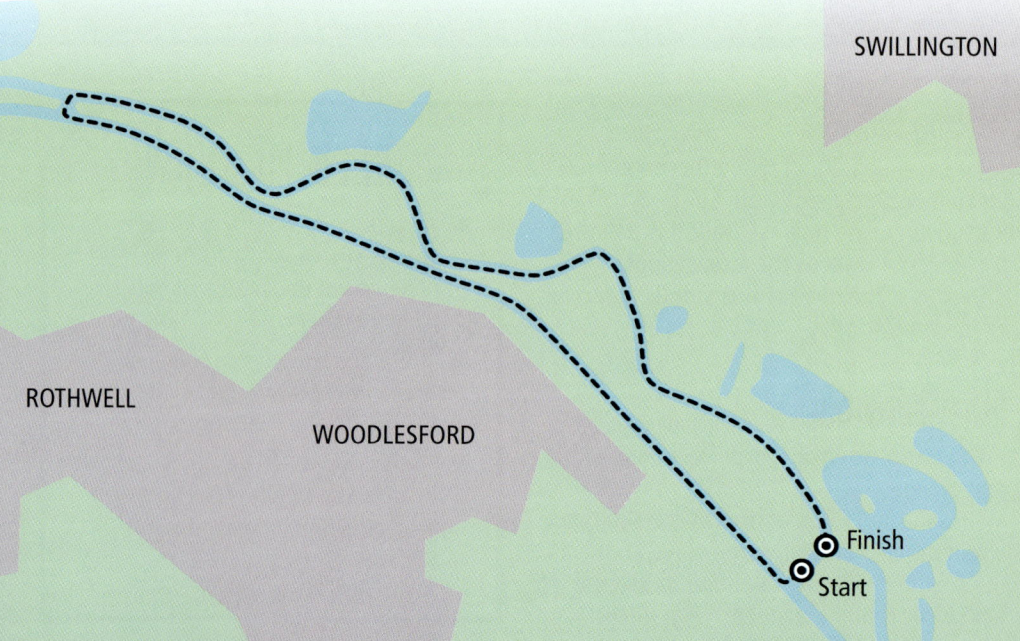

SWILLINGTON

ROTHWELL

WOODLESFORD

Finish

Start

## A brief history

The Aire & Calder Navigation was constructed to connect Leeds to the Humber and the North Sea. One unique feature of this waterway was the introduction of 'Tom Puddings' in the 1860s – huge open containers for transporting coal. These containers were linked together and pushed along by tugs. Unlike many British canals, which have remained relatively unchanged, the Aire & Calder Navigation has been continuously upgraded, particularly through lengthening the locks to accommodate larger and longer vessels.

The name Woodlesford reflects its geographical and historical features, deriving from the old English 'Wudu' meaning wood and 'Hirsaford', referring to a 'ford by the brushwood'. Old maps suggest the original ford was likely located on a dried-up bend of the River Aire near the present-day Woodlesford Lock.

## The paddle

The car park at Fleet Mills is ideally situated between the start and finish points of this paddle route. From the western side of the car park, head through the gate to find a small access jetty.

BELOW Woodlesford Circular from the air (credit Mike Blanshard).

Once on the water, bearing left would take you to Lemonroyd Waterside Marina and the start of the Aire & Calder Navigation. However, this route begins by heading right, taking you on to the canal. After a leisurely paddle of just under 2km, you'll reach Woodlesford Lock (No 5). Exit to the left for a short portage before re-entering the canal.

The next 1.5km is a peaceful paddle to Fishpond Lock (No 4). From here, you have a choice: either continue for a further 4km of uninterrupted canal into the heart of the city or turn around and retrace your path back along the canal to Fleet Mills. Both options promise a delightful experience on the water. However, if you are looking for a more exciting paddle, exit the water to the right and cross over on to the Rive Aire.

The river gets quite shallow in places so if you are on a SUP it's a good idea to change to a river fin before crossing over. Take a bit of care as you climb down the short bank to the river – it can be a little overgrown in summer or slippery in winter. It is also always important to check the river levels before embarking on the river section: normal levels are 40cm (check the Need to Know box overleaf).

Once on the water, you'll find yourself gliding along an ancient, winding stretch

of a naturally carved lazy river. After about a kilometre you will encounter the first set of gentle Grade I rapids at Leventhorpe. Beyond the rapids, tucked behind the trees, lie two local landmarks: Leventhorpe Hall, a Grade II listed building constructed in 1774, and Leventhorpe Vineyard. Established in 1985, the vineyard proudly reintroduced wine-growing to the region, after an absence of over 500 years.

Next up is Jango Island. Approaching the island, be sure to take the left-hand fork, otherwise you could find yourself snagging on some pretty sharp bushes. After 2.5km the river bends 90 degrees to the right and you pass under Swillington Bridge. Built in 1690, it holds the title of Leeds's oldest bridge. Take care when passing underneath as the flow can be quite fast.

From Swillington Bridge, it's another kilometre until the exit point at Fleet Lock (No 6). As the river bends to the right, you'll notice a concrete bank on the left with signs warning of a weir. The exit point is on the right, just before the concrete structure. Look for the stone remnants of the abandoned lock that once connected the canal to the river. A flat slab beneath the water makes getting out easier, but do take care as the riverbank can be a little slippery at times.

## NEED TO KNOW

■ The link for checking the water level on the River Aire is check-for-flooding.service.gov.uk/station/8061.

■ A waterways licence is needed to paddle the Aire & Calder Navigation. This can be obtained from the Paddle UK website: paddleuk.org.uk. Day or week passes can be purchased from the Canal & River Trust.

■ A river fin for SUP is needed for the return river section.

■ Be sure to exit the water before reaching the weir.

## Wildlife
Keep an eye out for kingfishers, kestrels, herons and swans.

## Food stops
Calilo Restaurant in Woodlesford is a Greek restaurant focusing on fresh ingredients and traditional recipes.

BELOW The launch spot (credit Mike Blanshard).

ABOVE Woodlesford Lock (credit Mike Blanshard).

## Getting there

• **By car** – From the A643 in Woodlesford, follow Fleet Lane for 2km. This brings you all the way into the car park.
• **By train** – The nearest train station is Woodlesford, easily reached from Leeds and Sheffield. From here, it's a 1.6km walk to the start.
• **By bus** – The nearest bus stop is opposite Woodlesford train station.

## Other activities

• If you are new to river paddling, consider having a specific river paddling lesson.

Mike Blanshard of **Paddle26** is a highly experienced local guide and instructor and uses this section of river for his 'introduction to river paddling' lessons. He can be contacted via his Facebook page Paddle26.
• For wine enthusiasts, a visit to **Leventhorpe Vineyard** is a must. Discover the rich history of winemaking in the region and enjoy a tasting experience featuring their range of wines. This is a working vineyard, so it's worth contacting them before visiting: info@leventhorpevineyard.co.uk.

# 29 RIVER DON – SPROTBROUGH TO MEXBOROUGH LOCK

Rising in the Pennines just west of Dunford Bridge, the River Don flows for 111km through the picturesque Don Valley before eventually joining the River Ouse near Goole. The scenic stretch from Sprotbrough Lock to Mexborough Lock offers a peaceful and sheltered paddle, showcasing the area's natural beauty. Along the route you can enjoy the abundant wildlife and quiet charm of the valley, making it an ideal escape into nature.

## The Lowdown

**DIFFICULTY**  ◗◗

**WATER TYPE**  River

**DISTANCE**  11km (round trip)

**PARKING**  Car park

**WHAT3WORDS**  ///clusters.ownership.tower

**LAUNCH**  Jetty

## A brief history
Sprotbrough to Mexborough forms part of the River Don Navigation, developed to improve navigation between Doncaster and Sheffield. The project began in 1726 with the construction of weirs and locks to help bypass the natural obstacles along the river. During the Industrial Revolution, the navigation played a crucial role in the

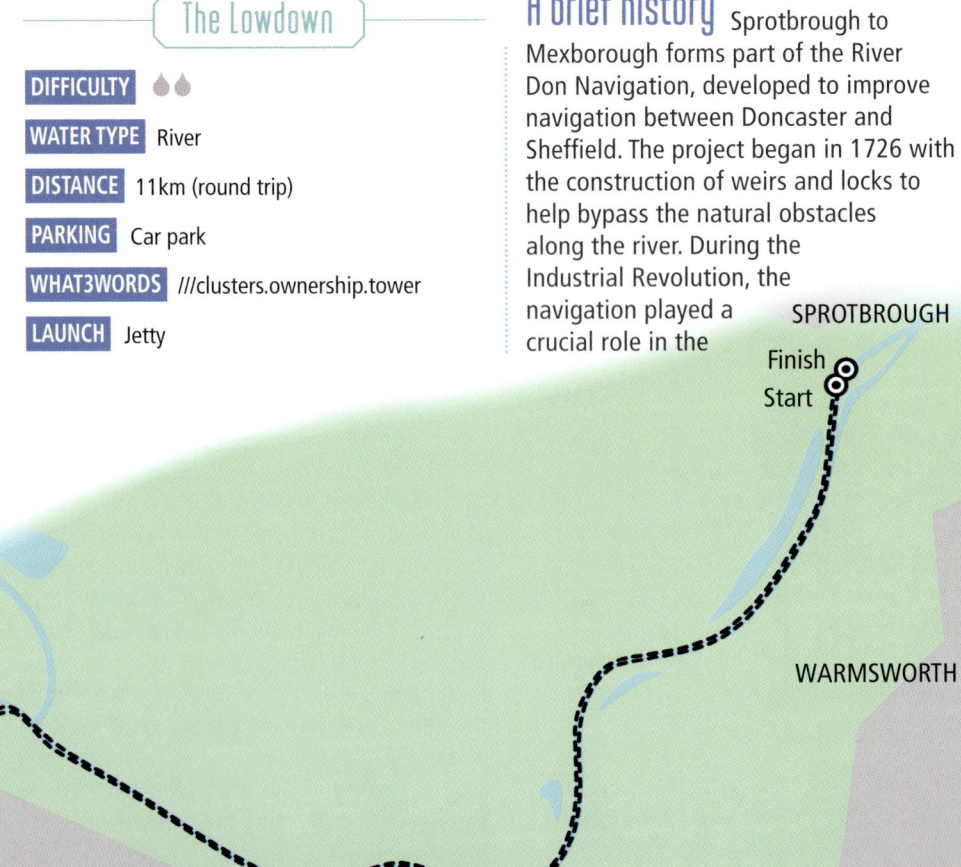

SPROTBROUGH

Finish

Start

WARMSWORTH

region's economic growth, transporting coal, steel, building materials and grain.

With the advent of the railways the navigation's importance started to decline, and today, while it may no longer be a major commercial route, the gentle moving water of the river is popular with recreational boaters and paddlers.

## The paddle
To reach the water, there is a gap in the trees at the lower end of the car park. If you're lucky and time it right, you can grab a quick drink from the artisan coffee cart that is often parked here. Once on the water, head in a southerly direction, passing the Boat Inn. The river here is nice and sheltered, making it a perfect relaxing paddle. You can meader through quiet, natural surroundings that provide plenty of opportunities to spot wildlife.

The journey continues upriver. After 2km, you pass beneath Rainbow Bridge; originally built in 1849 out of cast iron, it was replaced by the current steel construction

BELOW Ripples on the River Don.

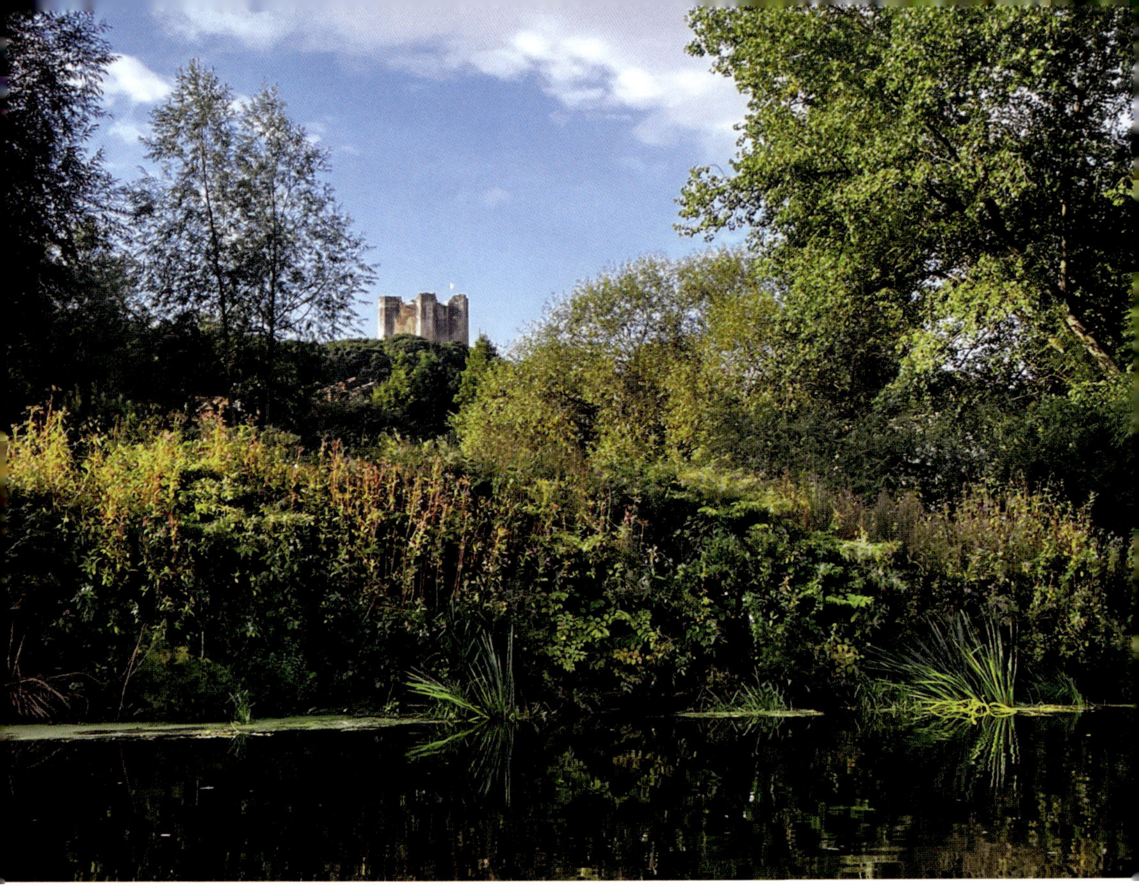

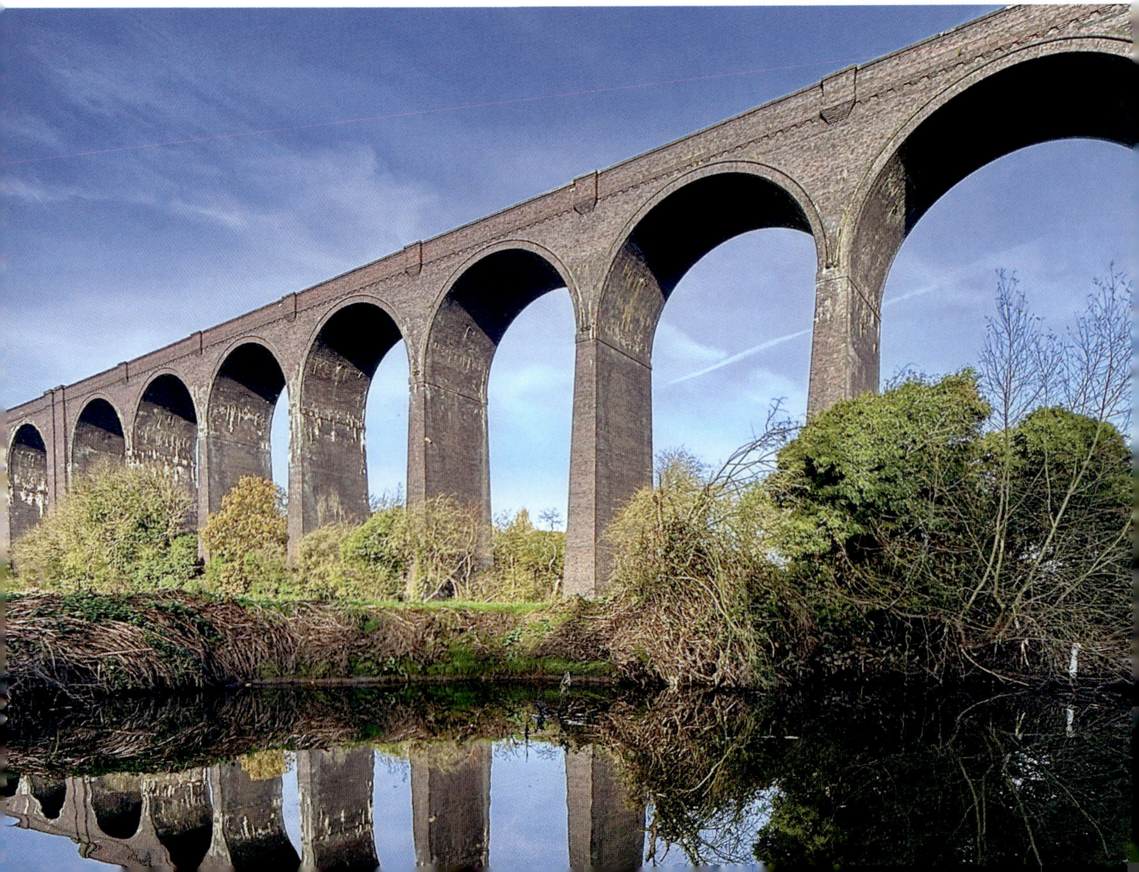

in 1928 to cope with increasingly heavier trains. Another kilometre along brings you to the impressive Conisbrough Viaduct. Opened in 1909, it has 21 arches and was built using 12 million Conisbrough blue bricks. The metal central span measures 46m long and 34m high. Originally built mainly to serve the coalfields, it closed in 1966 and today it forms part of the National Cycle Network. Shortly after the viaduct, through the trees on the right-hand side you can catch glimpses of the 11th-century Conisbrough Castle. From here, it's another 2km of peaceful tree-lined river passing under another rail bridge before you reach the Cadeby Colliery Bridge (No 57), given its name by the Canal & River Trust as it provided road access to the colliery. In 2004 it became the main access to the Earth Centre, an ambitious but short-lived eco-tourism project that is now a nature reserve and outdoor activity centre. Another kilometre brings you to Mexborough Lock. As you approach the lock, there is a little tributary river that you can explore; however, it's quite narrow, with plenty of overhanging trees, so be cautious if you are on a longer craft. The return to Sprotbrough is with the flow and as you approach the start point keep to the left-hand side to avoid the weir. It is well signposted and has a large orange barrier to help prevent anyone going further. Between the weir and the jetty is a picnic area, a perfect spot to relax after your paddle.

## Wildlife
Keep an eye out for otters and water voles along the riverbank. You can also expect to see moorhens, coots, kingfishers and herons while paddling this stretch of river.

## Food stops
The Boat Inn, adjacent to the river next to the start point, is a country pub with a full and hearty menu of pub classics and seasonal dishes. Enjoy a post-paddle pint in the beer garden during the summer or by the crackling log fire in the winter.

## Getting there
• By car – Exit the A1(M) at junction 36 on to the A630 towards Conisbrough. After approximately 1km, turn right on to Mill Lane and follow the road until you cross the river. Turn left on to Nursery Lane and the car park is on the left-hand side.
• By train – The nearest station is Doncaster, on the East Coast Main Line.
• By bus – The nearest bus stop is Sprotbrough Main Street, on the 219 route from Doncaster Interchange to Barnsley. From here, it's a 5-minute walk to the launch point.

## Other activities
• The Trans Pennine Trail walking route follows the river all the way from Sprotbrough through to Mexborough Lock.
• Conisbrough Castle has an impressive 27m (90ft) circular keep, the oldest surviving keep of its kind in England.

## NEED TO KNOW

■ There are toilets in the Boat Inn if you are grabbing a quick drink or snack.

■ You need a licence to paddle this stretch of water. This can be obtained from the Paddle UK website: paddleuk.org.uk.

TOP Conisbrough Castle peeking through the trees.

LEFT Conisbrough Viaduct reflecting in the water.

# THE NORTH WEST

Stretching from the cathedral city of Chester in the south to the university city of Lancaster in the north, and bordered by Cumbria, County Durham and Yorkshire, the North West of England is a region steeped in history, culture and natural beauty. Paddling into Chester, founded by the Romans in AD 79, offers a fascinating glimpse into the past with its ancient walls, amphitheatre and medieval architecture.

Further north, the industrial heritage of cities like Liverpool and Manchester highlights the region's transformation into a powerhouse during the Industrial Revolution. These large cities' waterways, including the Bridgewater and Leeds & Liverpool canals, offer paddlers a unique way to explore both urban vibrancy and rural tranquillity. The Leeds & Liverpool Canal in particular features several times throughout this book.

The coastline offers its own allure. From the sweeping dunes of the Sefton Coast to the wildlife-rich Morecambe Bay, the North West's coastal landscape, along with its sheltered marine lakes and estuaries, provides ideal locations to explore the diverse ecosystems and spot wildlife like seals and wading birds.

Whether gliding along canals, rivers or the open coastline, the North West offers a paddling experience as diverse as its landscapes, blending history, adventure and natural beauty.

ABOVE The first signs of autumn over Sprotbrough.

RIGHT Bridgewater Canal.

# 30 CARNFORTH TO LANCASTER

**Affectionately known as the 'Lanky',** the Lancaster Canal is the longest lock-free canal in England. Stretching 66km from Preston to Kendal, it's a slow, meandering canal with a mix of urban and open countryside, making it the perfect location for those taking up paddle sports for the first time or for some longer distance uninterrupted paddling.

## The Lowdown

**DIFFICULTY** 💧

**WATER TYPE** Canal

**DISTANCE** 11.5km (round trip)

**PARKING** Car park

**WHAT3WORDS** ///obstinate.tanks.wide

**LAUNCH** Bankside

## A brief history

Lancaster has a rich and interesting history and boasts many stories of ghoulish goings-on. In 1612, the trial of the Pendle Witches began in Lancaster Castle. It took three days to find a total of ten people guilty of witchcraft, and they were then executed on the moors overlooking the city. Is it any wonder the city became known as 'the Hanging Town'?

Originally intended to carry cargo from the coalfields of Westhoughton to Kendal, the section of the Lancaster Canal over the Ribble Valley was never

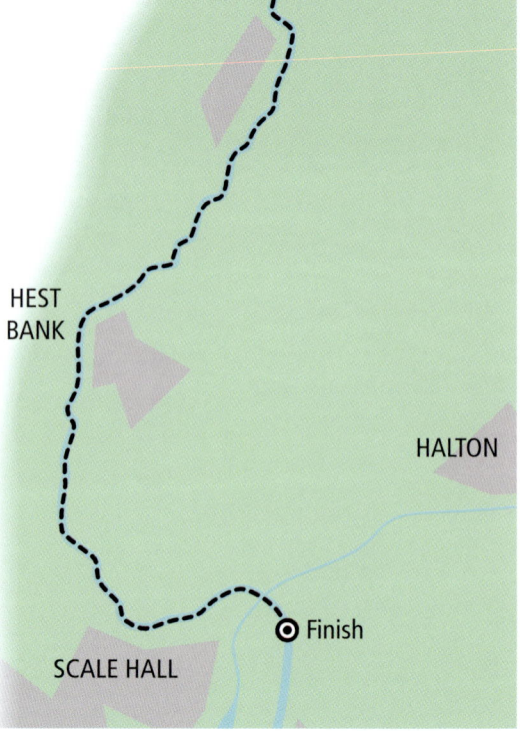

completed due to the cost of building a series of 32 locks and an aqueduct, leaving the northern section an isolated waterway. It wasn't until 2002 that the Ribble Link opened, finally connecting the canal to the English canal network.

## The paddle

Park in Detron Gate Farm lay-by and it's a short walk up the path to reach the canal. It's easier to access the water just before the bridge. Once on the water, head south away from the bridge towards Lancaster.

The canal passes through the village of Bolton-le-Sands and under five bridges before reaching the low Hatlex Swing Bridge. If you're lucky and time it right, a passer-by may open the bridge for you, otherwise you will have to portage around. It's quite easy to get out and only a short 20m walk to the other side. Approaching Hest Bank, don't be alarmed if you pass a cluster of skeletons enjoying afternoon tea; just look up and take in the spooktacular views over Morecambe Bay. The family of skeletons could be guarding the canal warehouse – it's one of the most picturesque buildings on the canal. Built in 1819 by the Hest Bank Canal Company, it was used to store goods brought up from the sea before loading on to barges for transport further up the canal. You can clearly see the access door seemingly leading straight out on to the water.

BELOW A narrowboat moored along the canal.

Leaving Hest Bank, you'll find more beautiful countryside, trees and humpback bridges before passing Skerton and eventually reaching the most outstanding landmark on the paddle. The Lune Aqueduct, holder of a National Transport Trust 'Red Wheel' plaque, carries the canal 202.4m, 18.6m above the River Lune. It's made up of five 21m arches, giving picture-perfect vistas over the Lune Valley.

There can be quite a breeze blowing through, so it's a good idea if you're paddling a SUP to kneel while passing over the aqueduct. From here, it's 2.5km to Lancaster and a lunch stop at the White Cross pub.

Approaching the city, the paddle becomes more and more urban. Soon, the towering spire of Lancaster Cathedral comes into view alongside the Grade II listed brick water tower of Moor Lane Mill, now converted into an office block. From here, it's only another 1km to the White Cross.

## Wildlife

As the canal winds through the fields, it's a common sight to see horses taking a drink from the canal water alongside moorhens, mute swans and kingfishers.

## Food stops

There are several pubs and restaurants sitting right on the canal-side that you can pull up alongside.
• At a little over 4km into the paddle, the Hest Bank pub can be a good pit stop on the way to the White Cross.
• The White Cross, the end destination of the paddle, is a furbished cotton mill on the bankside of the canal. It serves cask ales, beers and an excellent selection of wines. Their home cooked food is delicious. The menu does change with the seasons and if the time is right, my favourite is the dipping gravy served with the pork, leek and Welsh rarebit sausage sandwich – it is just divine!
• On the return journey, paddle 1km further past the lay-by to the town of Carnforth for the Canal Turn, a traditional English pub serving real ales and classic pub lunches.

## Getting there

• By car – From junction 35 of the M6, follow the B601 to Carnforth and from here take the A6 towards Lancaster. The car park is on the left-hand side, 400m after the town.
• By train – The nearest station is Carnforth, 2.5km from the paddle start car park.
• By bus – Denton Gate Farm bus stop is situated at the paddle start car park.

## Other activities

• The towpath runs the length of the canal and is suitable for walking and considerate cycling.
• CN Watersports, just north of Carnforth, offer lessons in waterskiing and wakeboarding as well as thrill rides on a speed boat.

ABOVE Hatlex Swing Bridge.

RIGHT Karen paddling between the bridges.

## NEED TO KNOW

■ There are no toilets available in the car park.

■ You need a licence to paddle on any canal in England. Licences can be obtained from the Paddle UK website, paddleuk.org.uk.

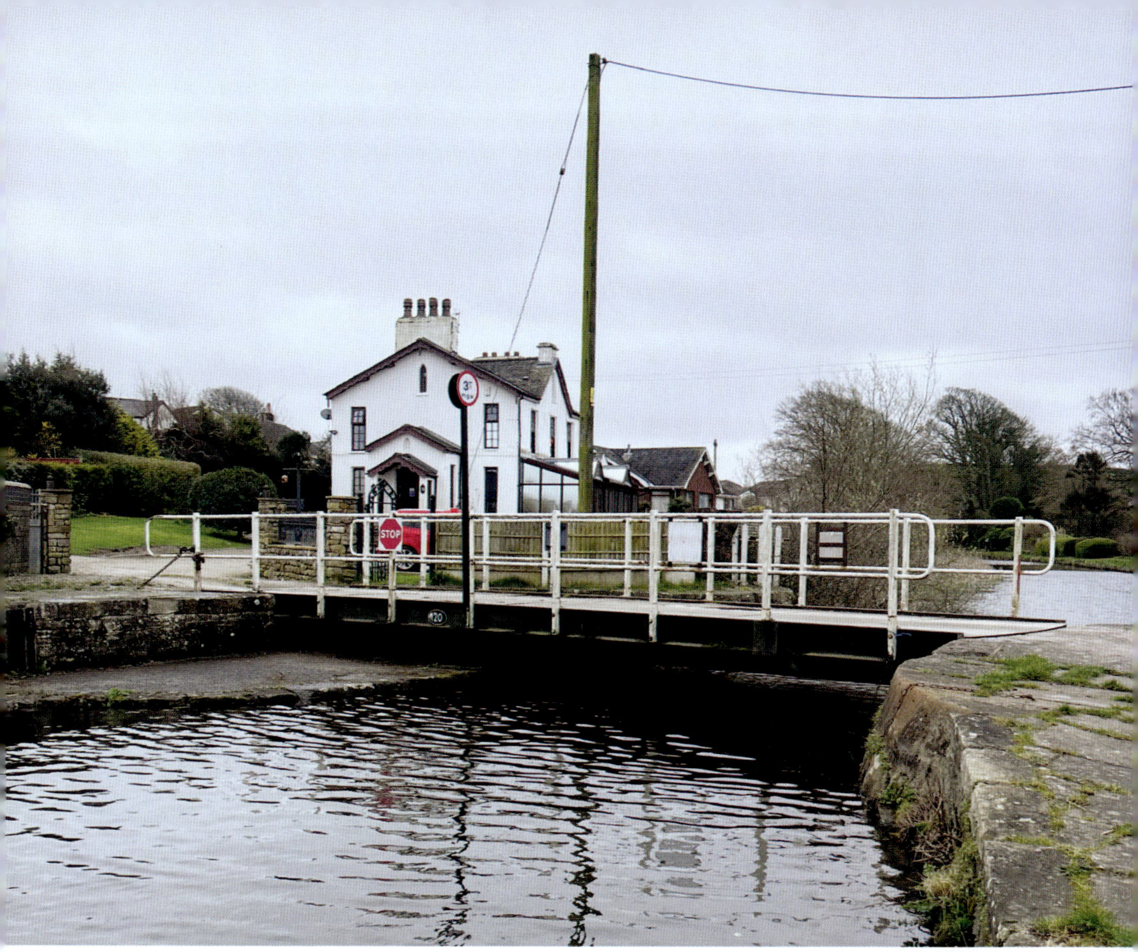
STOP

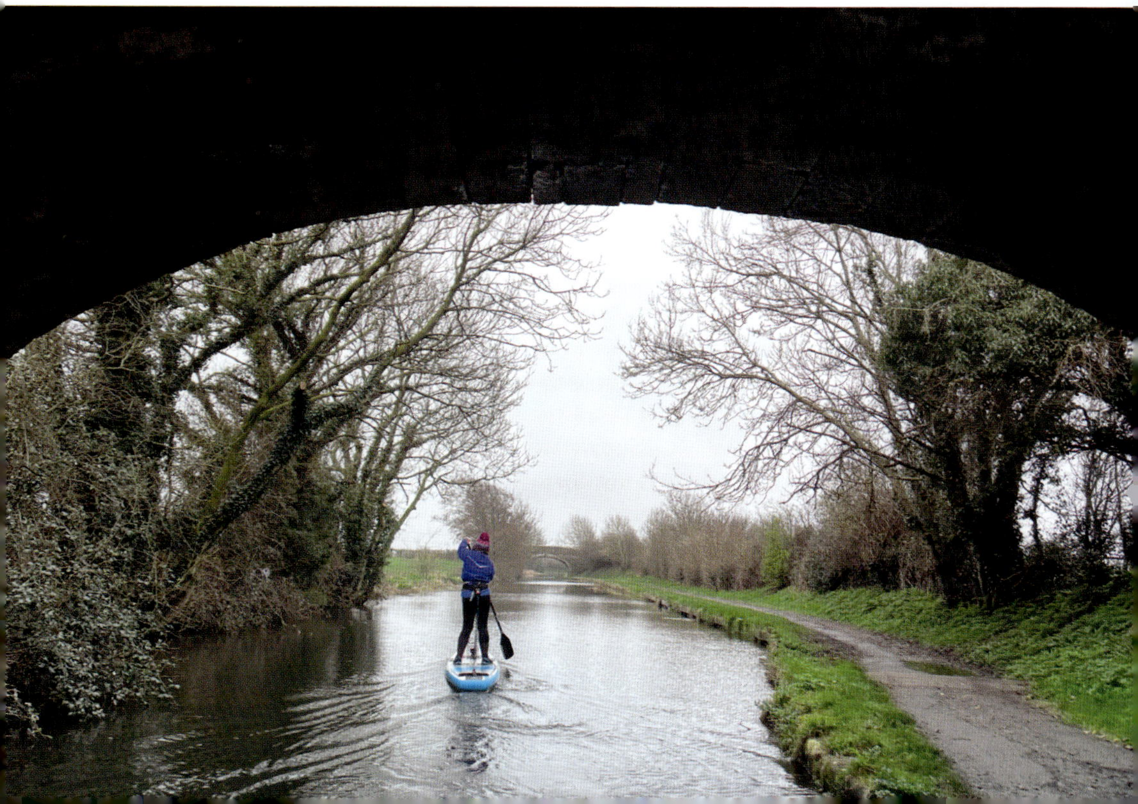

# 31 FOULRIDGE TUNNEL

Embark on an unforgettable adventure of light, shadow and 'tunnel tears' while navigating this cool damp passageway that's rich in history and atmosphere. Every stroke takes you deeper into a captivating journey back in time. A must-do for every paddle enthusiast.

## The Lowdown

**DIFFICULTY** 

**WATER TYPE** Canal

**DISTANCE** 5km (round trip)

**PARKING** Car park

**WHAT3WORDS** ///corrode.pacifist.hints

**LAUNCH** Canal towpath

## A brief history

Known as the Mile Tunnel, the Foulridge Tunnel is actually slightly short of a mile at 1,630 yards (1,490m) long. It's 21m underground and is the longest tunnel in the country that is freely open for canoes, kayaks and SUPs to navigate. Built in the 18th century by Samuel Fletcher as part of the Leeds & Liverpool Canal, the tunnel is almost 150m above sea level and is the highest point on the 204km-long canal. As there is no towpath inside the tunnel, the bargemen used to push the barges through by lying on their backs and walking their feet along the roof of the tunnel, while their horses were led over the top. There are reports that in September 1912, a cow fell into the canal near the western portal and swam the length of the tunnel before being helped out and revived with brandy!

## The paddle

The Foulridge Tunnel operates on a traffic light system. The lights go green on the hour at the Foulridge end. They stay green for 10 minutes before returning to red. If you depart at the top of the hour, this gives you 30 minutes to reach the other end. At the western portal, the lights go green on the half hour, and

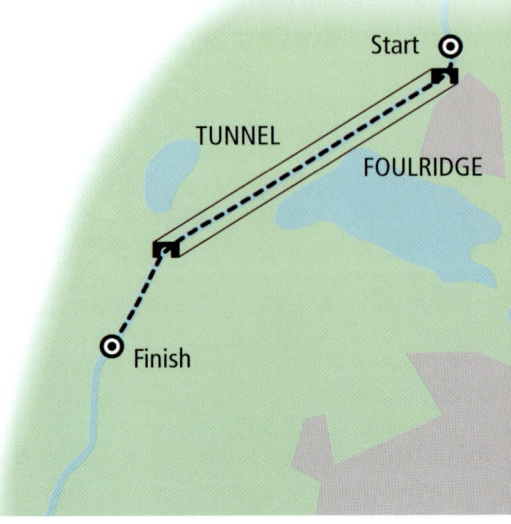

ABOVE Inside Foulridge Tunnel
(credit Mike Blanshard)

again stay green for 10 minutes. A forward-facing bright white light personal flotation device with attached whistle is a must when undertaking this paddle.

Launching from the Wharf at Foulridge, it's only 250m to the start of the tunnel, so it's a good idea to check the time first. The cafe is open for breakfasts and serves takeaway coffee if you are a little early. As you approach the tunnel, if you line up with the centre and look through you can see the light at the other end. Before entering, always double-check to make sure nothing is coming towards you.

As you move through and lose the light from behind, you must now rely on the torch you brought with you. You can hear the echoes of the 'tunnel tears', a natural phenomenon where groundwater seeps through the porous sections of the tunnel. This is perfectly normal, and if you look closely at the ceiling, you can see the mineral deposits left behind, forming stalactites. As you continue, there are three ventilation shafts; these help to keep the air circulating as well as providing a little ambient light. You may notice signs along the wall with numbers on. These indicate the distance in yards you have left to paddle.

Once out the other side, it's 500m to Bridge 145, otherwise known as the Wanless packhorse bridge, which was built

in 1794 as a vital crossing point to transport goods. You can exit the water here on the left-hand side, cross over and head to Greenwoods Farmhouse Kitchen for a bite to eat before returning to Foulridge.

## Wildlife

The tunnel is a cold and dark place – perfect for some species of **bats** to hide and search for prey, so don't be surprised if you see one flying past.

## Food stops

This route is sandwiched between two food stops.
- **Fabellos**, located at the Wharf at Foulridge, serves traditional Italian cuisine with a modern twist. It opens from 10am for hot and cold refreshments, and serves meals from noon.
- Next to Bridge 145 is the **Greenwoods Farmhouse Kitchen**.

## Getting there

- **By car** – Foulridge is situated 13km north east of Burnley on the A56. Once in Foulridge, follow signs for the Wharf.
- **By train** – The nearest train station is Colne, on the East Lancashire (Preston to Colne) Line.
- **By bus** – The nearest bus stop is Skipton

ABOVE The exit of Foulridge Tunnel.

Road – from here it's a short walk to the start point. Take either the M4 or M5 bus from Colne.

## Other activities
The **Walking with Witches Trail** starts at the Barley car park at the foot of Pendle Hill. This is a self-guided walking trail that follows the route the Pendle Witches took through the Ribble Valley to Lancaster Castle, where they stood trial for witchcraft. Download the route from the Visit Lancashire website: www.visitlancashire.com.

# 32 FAIRHAVEN LAKE

With a potentially long walk to the sea and challenging conditions like strong winds, currents and tides, the Fylde coastline can be a difficult place to paddle. Fairhaven Lake offers the perfect alternative. This tranquil saltwater lake, one of only a handful of marine lakes in Britain, is surrounded by picturesque parkland and abundant wildlife. Though small, Fairhaven Lake is a gem, offering a fun-filled day for the entire family.

## The Lowdown

**DIFFICULTY** 💧

**WATER TYPE** Lake

**DISTANCE** Variable (1.6km circumference)

**PARKING** Parking bays at side of road

**WHAT3WORDS** ///yesterday.mows.admiral

**LAUNCH** Jetty

## A brief history

Fairhaven Lake Gardens were created in the 1890s as part of a seaside development to boost tourism and create a high-class residential and leisure area between the urban districts of Lytham and St Annes. After the two districts merged in 1922, the lake and grounds were further extended, increasing the size of the park to 19.5ha and doubling the size of the lake to over 800m. In 2018, the site underwent a £2.9M renovation project, restoring the lake, gardens and buildings to their former glory.

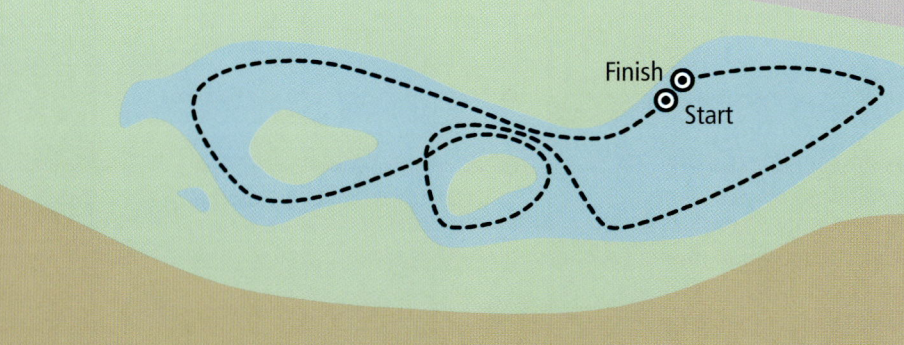

## The paddle

Launching from the jetty adjacent to the boat house, you are free to explore the entire lake. With a circumference of 1.6km and a depth of around 1.2m, it's a very safe environment for a beginner to learn and hone their skills, yet it offers plenty of opportunities for the experienced paddler. There are two islands towards the south-west of the lake that you can explore – just be aware that although you can paddle around them, landing on the islands is not permitted. This side of the lake tends to be more secluded. Further past the islands to the west end is the Lytham St Annes Spitfire Memorial, a life-size replica of a Second World War Spitfire W3644 that flies high in the sky, mounted on a 3m pole. If you're on the lake during the day, expect to share the water with other craft, including the motorboats that are available to hire. Their speed is limited, though, so they don't give off any real wash that could catch you out.

## Wildlife

The nutrient-dense **Ribble Estuary** attracts hundreds of thousands of birds each year. On the lake itself you will see **Canada geese**, **swans**, **coots** and **mallards** gracing the surface, while **tufted ducks** are diving underwater looking for their food.

## Food stops

• **The Lakeside café**, situated adjacent to the boat house, has a wide selection of hot and cold food, cakes and ice creams.
• **The Greek Flame Taverna** in Lytham St Annes serves up a traditional Greek dining experience.

## Getting there

• **By car** – Follow the A5230 to the coast. At the T-junction, turn left onto Clifton Drive North. Follow for 5km towards Lytham. The lake is well signposted on the right-hand side.
• **By train** – The nearest train station is Ansdell & Fairhaven on the Blackpool South to Preston line. From the station, it is half a mile to the lake.
• **By bus** – The nearest bus stop is Lake Road North, the 76 bus on the Blackpool to St Annes route. From here, it's a 3-minute walk to the lake.

BELOW A footpath alongside Fairhaven Lake.

## Other activities

The park offers a host of activities including a children's play area, a skate park, crazy golf, bowling and both lawn and hard surface tennis courts. Further afield, the Blackpool Illuminations are on display from late August until November. For me, a trip to Lytham St Annes wouldn't be complete without a visit to Lowther Gardens to see the statue of the greatest comedian of all time, Bobby Ball.

### NEED TO KNOW

■ There is a small fee to use the lake – a permit to paddle can be purchased from the boating kiosk. It is free to paddle on Wednesday evenings.

■ There are toilets and changing facilities on site.

■ Landing on the islands is prohibited.

LEFT A gaggle of Canada geese.

BELOW The Spitfire Memorial.

# 33 PARBOLD TO WIGAN PIER – LEEDS & LIVERPOOL CANAL

The Leeds & Liverpool Canal is the longest canal in Britain, stretching 204km across the Pennines and connecting the bustling city of Leeds to the vibrant docks of Liverpool. Paddle from Parbold to Wigan to experience picturesque countryside intertwined with remnants of the canal's industrial past. Glide through serene waters, passing under historic stone bridges and traditional locks, while enjoying the abundant wildlife and peaceful surroundings.

## The Lowdown

**DIFFICULTY** 

**WATER TYPE** Canal

**DISTANCE** 11km (one way)

**PARKING** Car park

**WHAT3WORDS** ///glimmers.conceals.dome

**LAUNCH** Canal-side

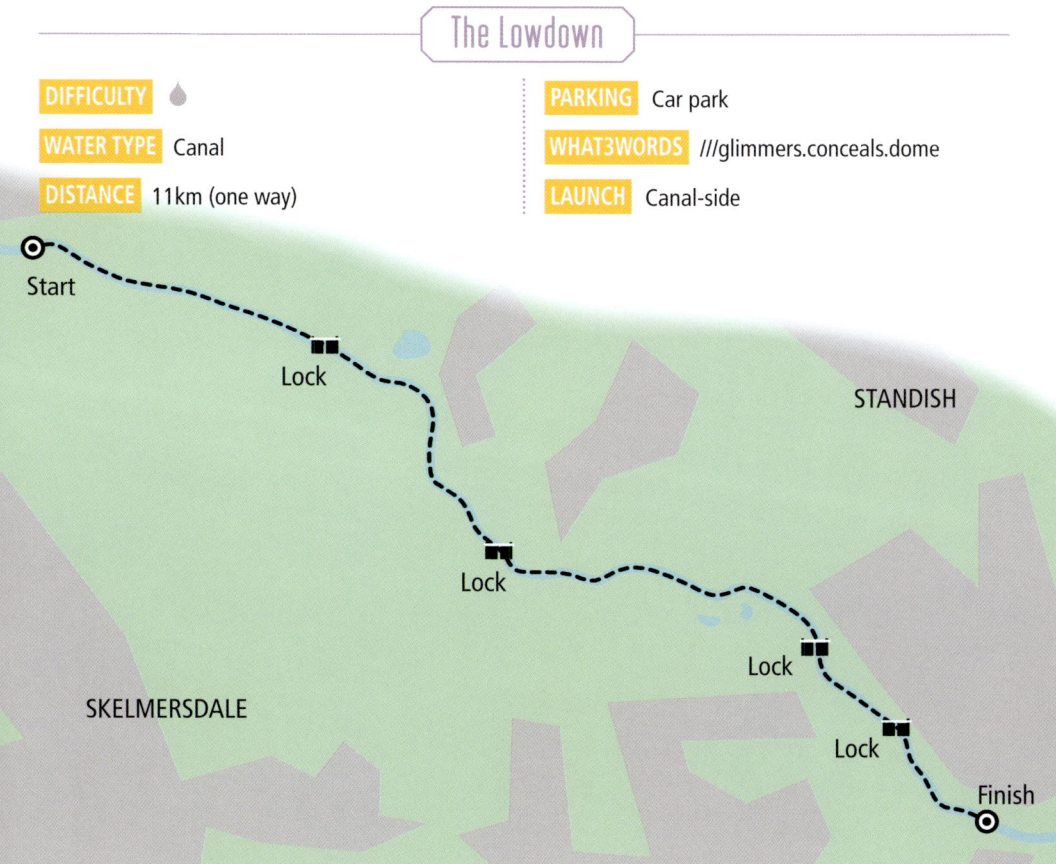

Start

Lock

STANDISH

Lock

Lock

SKELMERSDALE

Lock

Finish

## A brief history

The village of Parbold developed from a few scattered agricultural settlements along the River Douglas. Its growth was accelerated with the introduction of the Douglas Navigation in 1742, followed by the Leeds & Liverpool Canal, which reached Wigan around 40 years later. Notably, the Leeds & Liverpool Canal was the first of the Trans-Pennine canals to commence construction, yet it was the last to be completed. The intricate route and considerable distance led to a lengthy 46-year building process, ultimately costing five times more than initially estimated.

## The paddle

The car park can fill up quite quickly, particularly during the summer months, so it's worth getting there early. Opposite the car park is the Parbold Windmill, originally built in 1794 as a corn mill. Over time, the sails were removed and today the building is used as a gallery studio. Once on the water, head east. Passing under the bridge, you come to a sharp right bend, at Parbold Dry Dock. The dock was part of the original route of the canal before construction was halted and re-routed towards Blackburn and Burnley. As you pass under the many bridges that cross the canal, look out for deep gouges carved into the stonework. In the canal's early days, boats were towed by horses walking along the towpath with long ropes. As the ropes passed over the stone edges, they gradually wore them away.

At the 3km mark you reach Appley Lock (No 91); this is the first of four portages along the route. Exit via the low wall on the right-hand side. A further kilometre along, you reach Finch Mill Swing Bridge (No 43). This is a low bridge, and you may need to kneel and crouch down as you pass under. Alternatively, you can portage around if you

LEFT If you look closely, you can see where the ropes have worn away the stone.

BELOW Andy Smith gliding
along the canal.

prefer. Approaching Dean Lock (No 90) after 6km, you can see the remains of a lock that used to take boats from the canal to the Douglas Navigation. This was a canalised section of the River Douglas but was bought out by the Liverpool Leeds Canal Company in 1772.

Exit the water on the right-hand side next to the lock keeper's house. On the other side of the lock, the canal passes under the M6 motorway before winding its way through the trees and countryside, passing Crooke Marina. After 3km you come to Ell Meadow Lock (No 89). Take care on the other side as there is a longer drop to the water. From here, the scenery becomes more industrial and ahead you can make out the arch of the Brick Community Stadium, home to both Wigan Warriors rugby club and Wigan Athletic football club. Pagefield Lock (No 88), opposite the stadium, is the last portage before you arrive at Wigan Pier. Despite its name, Wigan Pier is not a seaside tourist attraction, but was in fact a coal-loading staithe where wagons would tip their loads on to waiting barges. The remains of the tipper can be seen opposite the Wigan Pier warehouse building. Turn right under the No 51 bridge and you can exit the water via the jetty on the left-hand side.

## Wildlife

Kingfishers, known for being very territorial, are often spotted between bridges 41 and 43, so keep an eye out. Herons, swans and mallards are also regular visitors to the canal.

## Food stops

• The Windmill at Parbold is a traditional country pub that prides itself on using local produce. It changes the menu with the seasons to keep it fresh and interesting.
• Feast at The Mills on Swan Meadow Road, opposite Wigan Pier, is a street

## NEED TO KNOW

■ A licence is needed to paddle on the canal. This can be purchased from the Paddle UK website: paddleuk.org.uk.

■ There are no toilets or changing facilities at the car park.

food festival held every Friday evening and Saturday and Sunday from midday. It features local and international cuisine, live entertainment and craft drinks.

## Getting there

• By car – From M6 junction 27, follow the A5209 into Parbold village and turn right into Mill Lane. Cross the bridge and the car park is immediately on your left.
• By train – Parbold is on the Manchester to Southport Line. From the station, it's a 5-minute walk to the car park.
• By bus – Catch the 312 from Ormskirk. The bus stop is near the train station and only a 5-minute walk to the launch spot.

## Other activities

The towpath runs parallel to the canal, making it perfect for walking and cycling.

ABOVE The old Trencherfield Mill at Wigan Pier.

# 34 SOUTHPORT MARINE LAKE

A tranquil oasis by the sea, Southport Marine Lake is one of the largest man-made lakes in the UK. Covering 56ha, with a length of 1.6km, a width of 400m and a depth of around 1.2m, it's the perfect setting for a peaceful paddling experience.

## The Lowdown

**DIFFICULTY**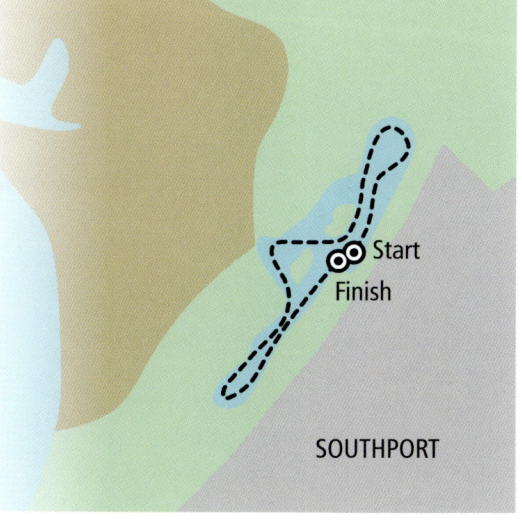

**WATER TYPE**  Lake

**DISTANCE**  Variable (3.5km circumference)

**PARKING**  Southport Watersports Centre car park

**WHAT3WORDS**  ///settle.librarian.dizzy

**LAUNCH**  Jetty

Start
Finish

SOUTHPORT

## A brief history

Built on reclaimed foreshore, Southport Marine Lake and the adjoining King's Gardens were opened in 1887 as part of a series of leisure developments along the seafront. The goal was to help capitalise on Southport's growing popularity as a Victorian holiday destination and transform the town into a premier seaside resort. As the town expanded and the sea receded, the lake was extended multiple times to compensate for the increasing difficulty in accessing seawater, ensuring it remained a key attraction for visitors.

The expansive sands of Southport beach also became a prime training ground for racehorses, including the legendary Red Rum, the only horse to win the Aintree Grand National three times.

## The paddle

Access the water from the jetty at Southport Watersports Centre – there is no need to check in, and there are no time restrictions on your paddling. However, when motorboats and pedalos are operating, paddling is restricted to the area north of the pier. The bowl at the far north end of the lake, beyond the breakwater, is

ABOVE Peter and Bruce by Marine Way Bridge.

reserved for water-skiers, and while you're allowed to paddle there, you are kindly asked to move out if any skiers arrive. The circumference of the lake is 3.5km, with plenty of things to explore along the way.

The two islands in the centre of the lake were created during the 1963 extension. Part of the original sea wall was left intact during the expansion, saving both time and money, while also creating a valuable habitat for wildlife. The bowl area to the north was added in a further extension three years later. Moving along the lake, behind the islands is Southport Sailing Club and the West Lancashire Yacht Club, who can be seen regularly on the water all year round. Further south, you reach what appear to be three bridges. The first is the impressive cable-stayed Marine Way, a suspension bridge, built in 2004 to replace the old cast-iron one, which closed in 1990. The large structure behind is not actually a

bridge but in fact Southport Pier, spanning the lake and stretching out into the Irish Sea. It opened in 1860 and at 1,108m, it is Britain's second-longest pier. The last bridge you come to is the Venetian Bridge. Built in 1931, it has three spans and was designed to link the promenade with King's Gardens.

Overlooking the south side of the lake is the unmissable Southport Big Wheel, which stands 35m tall and provides stunning views over the lake. During the summer months you may see SUP North out on the water, either carrying out lessons or conducting training sessions. On a Friday evening during the summer, they host a paddle and pint social evening where they finish their paddle at the Lakeside Inn, which for many years held the Guinness world record as the smallest pub in Britain.

## Wildlife
Populations of Canada geese and mute swans have made the lake their home. Also keep an eye out while paddling past the islands, as they are host to a small colony of egrets.

## Food stops
• The Lakeside Inn next to the watersports centre may be the small, but it has a fully stocked bar, toilets and serves freshly made pork pies – they are amazing!
• Marine Lake Café beside the pier serves quality British food, ice cream and hot and cold drinks.

## Getting there
• By car – At the junction of the A570 with Lord Street, turn right then left onto Nevill Street. At the T-Junction, turn right on to the promenade and the watersports centre is on the left-hand side.
• By train – The nearest train station is Southport, 800m from the watersports centre.
• By bus – The nearest bus stop is Leicester St/Promenade. Take the 40 bus operated by Merseytravel.

## Other activities
• Southport Model Railway Village, located to the south of the lake, is a model village with a difference. The attraction is designed with the rail enthusiast in mind. If you or your children enjoy watching trains, this is the place for you.
• Golf enthusiasts, you are on the 'Golf Coast'! There is a host of world-class courses. Royal Birkdale, host to multiple open championships, is located just to the south of the town.

## NEED TO KNOW

■ You need a licence to paddle on the lake. Day licences can be obtained from the Southport Marine Lake website: www.southportmarinelake.com.

■ There are no toilet or changing facilities in the car park.

BELOW Boards lined up post-paddle outside the Lakeside Inn.

# 35 WALLASEY TO LEASOWE BEACH

Experience the thrilling waves or silky-smooth seas of the Wirral, a region rich in history and industrial heritage. Venture north and the towering cranes of the Liverpool docks dominate the skyline, a testament to the area's vibrant maritime legacy. Head south to discover expansive sand dunes that stretch along the coast – the area is a sanctuary for migrating birds and diverse sea-life. The Wirral offers a unique blend of natural beauty and historical intrigue.

## The Lowdown

**DIFFICULTY** ◆◆◆

**WATER TYPE** Sea

**DISTANCE** 5km

**PARKING** Wallasey Beach car park

**WHAT3WORDS** ///landed.pines.spite

**LAUNCH** Beach

## A brief history

During the 17th and 18th centuries, horse races were organised for the earls of Derby on the expansive sands at Leasowe; it is believed that these races were the forerunners of the modern-day Derby. It is said that 200 years ago the area was also a haven for pirates and smugglers, who used caves and tunnels carved through the soft sandstone

Start

Finish

WALLASEY VILLAGE

to dump and hide their contraband. There are reports that some of the caves were used in the transport of prisoners and slaves. During the Second World War, the tunnels were used as air-raid shelters and a munitions factory. Today, many of the tunnels have been blocked up, but guided tours are available to see the munitions factory.

## The paddle

The tidal range at Wallasey is the second largest in the UK, so I would recommend only paddling here one hour either side of high tide.

From Wallasey Beach car park, walk over the promenade and down the steps on to the sand. When the conditions allow, the shallow gradient of the beach provides gentle spilling waves and makes for a perfect opportunity to play and practise some SUP surfing. Looking over to your right you can see the mouth of the River Mersey and the formidable red and white tower cranes at Liverpool docks.

BELOW Ready for a paddle with SUP Wirral.

When you are ready to move on, follow the coastline and promenade away from the cranes, heading towards the Grade II listed Leasowe Lighthouse in the distance. Built in 1763 by the Mersey Docks and Harbour Company to guide shipping safely to the Port of Liverpool, it is the oldest surviving brick-built lighthouse in the UK. Decommissioned in 1908, the tower is now open to the public for guided tours.

You soon reach a strip of rocks, which form part of the sea defences, and once past the rocks you have reached the golden sands of Leasowe Beach. This is another gorgeous gentle sloping beach perfect for a play in the small waves, before returning to Wallasey. As you approach Wallasey beach, you can't help but be impressed by the industrial scale of the docks on the banks of the famous Mersey River.

## Wildlife

During autumn, if the conditions are right the Wirral peninsula is one of the best places in the west to spot a Leach's petrel. Although rare, seals and dolphins are occasionally spotted out at sea.

## Food stops

• Adjacent to the car park at Wallasey beach is the Derby Pool, a family-friendly pub and restaurant open for breakfast, lunch and dinner.
• The Marino Lounge on King's Parade, New Brighton, is a dog-friendly restaurant with views over Marine Lake. I can highly recommend the shakshuka with chorizo – it's simply delicious.

## Getting there

• By car – From the A554, turn on to Bayview Drive, which brings you to the car park for Wallasey beach.
• By train – The nearest station is Wallasey Grove Road, on the Wirral Line operated by Merseyrail. The station is 1.6km from Wallasey beach.
• By bus – The nearest bus stop is Wallasey Grove Road, opposite the train station.

## Other activities

• SUP Wirral, based in New Brighton, offer coastal SUP lessons on Wallasey beach and the calm flat waters of their own exclusive dock. They also hold SUP polo sessions throughout the winter.

ABOVE Andrew catching a little wave at Leasowe Beach.

• Mersey Tunnel Tour offer a tour of the famous Queensway Mersey Tunnel. It lasts approximately 2 hours and can be booked through tours@merseytravel.gov.uk.
• With 12 golf courses on the Wirral, there are plenty of options for all abilities, the most famous being the Royal Liverpool Golf Club, which has hosted the Open Championship.

## NEED TO KNOW

■ The tidal range at Wallasey is huge, so experience of coastal paddling is essential. Keep to an hour either side of high tide and check weather and sea state forecasts before undertaking this paddle.

■ There are toilets available in the Harvester restaurant for customers.

■ Both Wallasey and Leasowe beaches are RNLI lifeguarded from June to September.

# 36 LIVERPOOL ROYAL ALBERT DOCK

Paddling around Liverpool's Albert Dock offers a unique perspective of one of the city's most iconic areas. You will quickly notice the bustling atmosphere of the modern bars, restaurants and shops blending with the historic buildings and sights that surround this former UNESCO designated World Heritage Site.

## The Lowdown

**DIFFICULTY** ⬤

**WATER TYPE** Sea dock

**DISTANCE** Variable (5km circumference)

**PARKING** Liverpool Watersports Centre car park

**WHAT3WORDS** ///half.slides.august

**LAUNCH** Jetty

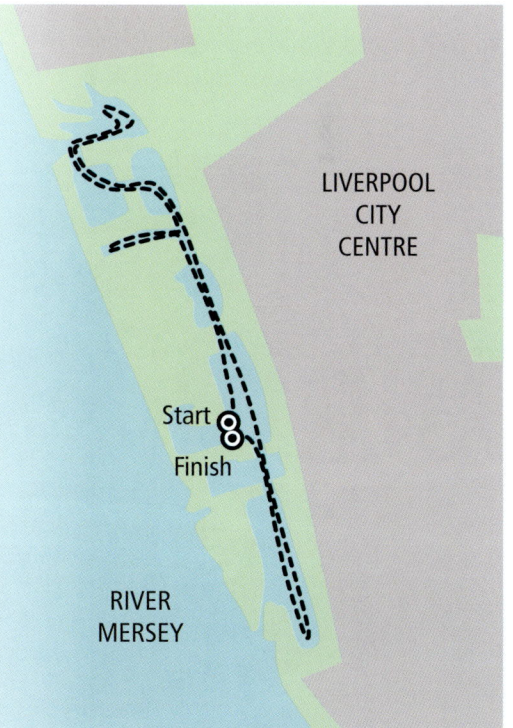

## A brief history

The Albert Dock was opened by Prince Albert in 1846 (it acquired its 'Royal' status 172 years later). It revolutionised the Liverpool docks forever, with its new secure and fireproof warehouses and new hydraulic cranes capable of lifting huge loads, significantly reducing the turnaround times of ships. The docks flourished until the advent of container ships in the late 20th century. This led to the closure of the dock in 1972. It was shuttered off and soon began filling with silt, until the south docks were almost covered.

A £100m regeneration scheme started in 1982 to transform the docks and buildings. The silt was dredged clear, and the warehouses transformed into a mix of commercial, leisure and residential facilities. The redevelopment was officially opened by HRH The Prince of Wales in 1988.

## The paddle

You can pre-book parking through the Liverpool Watersports Centre website: liverpoolwatersports.org.uk. From the car park, head up the ramp to the reception and they will give you a safety briefing and a quick guide to the docks before you get on the water. Kayaks, canoes, SUPS and swan pedalos are available for hire.

The docks are a combination of eight docks linked together, and you generally have permission to explore them all. Some of the highlights you will encounter include the Albert Dock warehouses. They were constructed between 1841 and 1846 and were among the first buildings in Britain to be made from cast iron, brick and stone. Devoid of any structural wood, they were designed to be fireproof.

As you make your way into Canning Dock, you are treated to some spectacular views of the famous Royal Liver Building. This Grade I listed building is one of the 'Three Graces', the other two being the Cunard Building and the Port of Liverpool Building. With its towering chimney, the Pump House is another unmissable landmark. Built in 1878 to provide power to cranes and hoists along the docks, today the Pump House has been converted to a pub and restaurant. Nestled in the corner of the Albert Dock is the Liverpool Mountain, a brightly coloured rock hammer-like sculpture by Swiss artist Ugo Rondinone that appears to defy gravity. It's just one of many art exhibits outside the Tate Liverpool art gallery.

Adjacent to Duke's Dock is the Wheel of Liverpool, a 60m-high Ferris wheel with fully enclosed capsules that provide some spectacular views over the city.

BELOW Sarah and Bruce at the Royal Albert Dock (credit Andrew Guthrie).

ABOVE The Royal Liver Building.

These are just a few of my highlights from paddling around Liverpool's Albert Dock. Whether you are local or a visitor, this paddle provides a unique and engaging way to experience Liverpool's maritime heritage.

## Wildlife

Don't be afraid if you notice any jellyfish in the water – they are moon jellyfish, the most common species in Britain, and are harmless, without any sting.

## Food stops

• Fika at the Waterfront is located above the watersports centre. Enjoy a coffee or a snack while taking in the amazing views over the docks.
• The Quayside Café on the ground floor of the Merseyside Maritime Museum on Hartley Quay serves hot and cold meals, teas and coffees. The views are stunning.

## Getting there

• By car – Liverpool Watersports Centre is located on Mariners Wharf, between Coburg Dock and Queen's Dock.
• By train – The nearest station is Liverpool Lime Street.
• By bus – The nearest bus stop is Mariners Wharf. Take the Merseytravel buses 4/4A.

## Other activities

• As well as paddle sports, the watersports centre aims to offer activities for everyone and includes a wheelchair accessible powerboat that allows anyone to enjoy the beauty of Liverpool's docks from the water. Also, why not take on the challenge of the Aqua Park inflatable obstacle course? Buoyancy aids and soft helmets are provided by the watersports centre.
• Wandering around the docks, you will encounter many attractions such as the Tate, the Big Wheel and various boutiques.
• A trip to Liverpool would not be complete without a visit to the famous Cavern Club, the venue that launched The Beatles' career.

## NEED TO KNOW

■ There are toilets and changing facilities inside the watersports centre.
■ Buoyancy aids are mandatory when on the water.

# 37 FARNDON TO CHESTER – RIVER DEE

The River Dee in Cheshire epitomises everything you would expect from a meandering river. Slowly snaking its way through the remote Cheshire countryside, it marks the border between England and Wales before finding its way into the heart of Chester. This is a longer paddle, so be prepared to be self-sufficient. However, the rewards are well worth the effort.

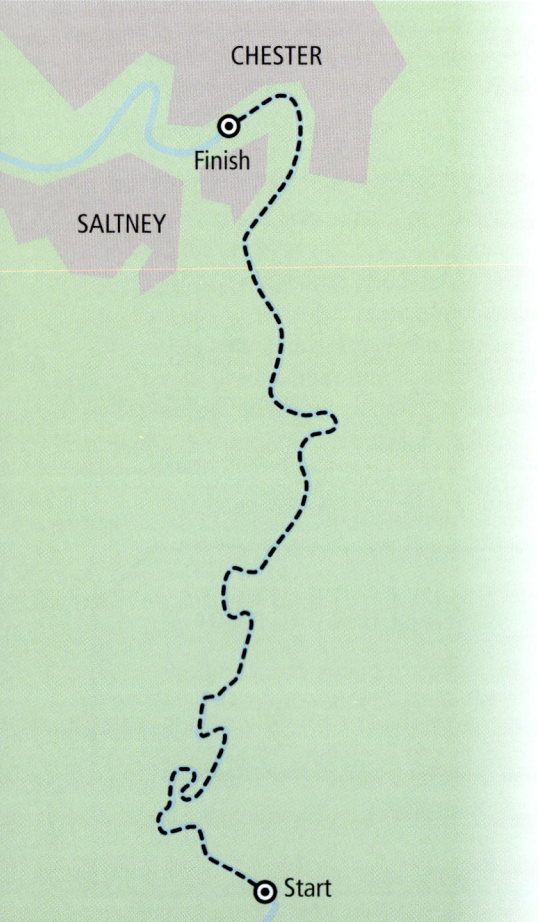

CHESTER

Finish

SALTNEY

Start

## The Lowdown

**DIFFICULTY** ♦♦ to ♦♦♦

**WATER TYPE** River

**DISTANCE** Up to 20km (one way)

**PARKING** Car park

**WHAT3WORDS** ///zoos.shocking.credited

**LAUNCH** Fishing peg

**A brief history** The main section of the River Dee stretches 113km, from Bala in North Wales through Chester before re-entering Wales. It is the only river in the UK to be covered by a Water Protection Zone. The city of Chester was founded as a Roman fortress in AD 79 and is one of Britain's best-preserved walled cities. Originally called Deva Victrix, it was a strategic stronghold for the Romans in the North West. Chester is also home to the largest Roman amphitheatre in Britain. After the Romans' withdrawal, Chester became a key Saxon settlement and later a Norman stronghold, evidenced by its impressive castle and cathedral. The medieval period saw Chester flourish as a market town. During Tudor times, a law was brought in dictating that Welshmen were banned from the city between sunset and sunrise.

## The paddle

From the car park at the side of the river, you can gain access to the water from one of the many fishing pegs along the bankside. Just take a little care as some can be quite steep. Once on the water, head north under the red sandstone Farndon Bridge, also known from the Welsh side as Holt Bridge. Built in the mid-14th century, this designated Grade I listed building is recorded in the National Heritage List for England and crosses the border between England and Wales. For the first 9km of this paddle, you will be straddling the border between the two countries.

The River Dee from Farndon slowly meanders its way through the fields and villages of the Cheshire countryside. Three kilometres in, you reach the only fast-moving section on the trip. It's Grade I at most, but if you're a little unsure then just go to your knees for around 100m until the

river returns to its slow and gentle pace. After approximately 11km you reach the blue and white cast-iron Aldford Iron Bridge. Designed by Thomes Telford for the 1st Marquis of Westminster, it was completed in 1824 and links the village of Aldford with Eaton Hall. Eaton Hall is the country house of the Duke of Westminster and covers 4,400ha of formal gardens, parkland, farmland and woodland. Today, the bridge is part of the Marches Way long-distance footpath.

At around 13km, where the river bends sharply to the left, you'll find a beach you can pull up in for a snack stop. You will reach Eccleston at 14.5km. If you are looking for a shorter paddle, there is a car park by the side of the river with another sandy beach, making for easy access and exit (///onlookers.split.comical). As you approach Chester, on the left is Sandy Lane Park and Aqua Park. This is an easy place to access and exit the river – you can end your

BELOW Andrew approaching the stunning Aldford Iron Bridge.

ABOVE The *Mark Twain* cruise boat.

RIGHT The start of the route through Farndon Bridge.

paddle here (///lights.award.covers) and catch the small ferry boat across the river to Queens Park. From Sandy Lane it's another 1.4km through the city of Chester. Pass under the historic Queens Park Suspension Bridge before finally exiting the water to the left, just before the weir and the Old Dee Bridge, and heading to one of the many cafés for some well-deserved post-paddle refuelling.

## Wildlife

Don't be surprised to find yourself sharing the water with cows and horses as they take a drink from the bankside. Herons, swans, moorhens, cormorants and kingfishers are just some of the birdlife that can be seen along the river.

## Food stops

• Snugburys on the River is a delicious ice-cream café sitting just below Queens Park Bridge in Chester. The Snugbury family have been making their own ice cream since 1986. The café also serves a selection of homemade sandwiches, cakes and pastries.
• Hickory's on Souters Lane is a family-friendly smokehouse serving BBQ favourites and smokehouse classics. They also pride themselves on their vegetarian and gluten-free menus.

## Getting there

• By car – Farndon lies 18km south of Chester, just off the A534. The car park is just after the bridge crossing the river.
• By train – The nearest train station is Chester, on the Wirral line.
• By bus – The nearest bus stop is in the village. Take the No 5 Stagecoach bus service from Chester.

## Other activities

• City Walls – Chester is the only city with its full circuit of defensive walls intact. Walking the complete circuit gives spectacular views of this historic city.
• Chester Zoo is so much more than just an animal park with more than 37,000 animals from over 520 species and 128 acres of zoological gardens. As a conservation and education charity, the zoo works tirelessly to help prevent extinction of wildlife throughout the world.
• The Rows are unique two-tiered medieval shopping galleries, housing a mix of boutique shops, cafés, bars and attractions.

## NEED TO KNOW

■ There are public toilets in the car park at the start of the paddle, just over the bridge.

# 38 BARTON SWING AQUEDUCT TO GIANT'S BASIN VIA OLD TRAFFORD

This is an urban paddle that takes you straight into the vibrant heart of Manchester. You will experience the city's iconic landmarks from a unique perspective, gliding over the impressive Barton Swing Aqueduct, before passing the legendary Old Trafford football stadium, then arriving in the bustling city centre where history and modern energy meet. It's an unforgettable paddle through Manchester's dynamic urban landscape.

## The Lowdown

**DIFFICULTY** 💧

**WATER TYPE** Canal

**DISTANCE** 11km (round trip)

**PARKING** Lay-by

**WHAT3WORDS** ///sparks.riches.export

**LAUNCH** Canal-side

## A brief history

The Bridgewater Canal was completed in 1761 and is regarded as England's first true still-water canal. It was a pioneering achievement of the Industrial Revolution, and was commissioned by Francis Egerton, the 3rd Duke of Bridgewater, and engineered by James Brindley. The canal was originally built to transport coal from the duke's mines in Worsley to Manchester. It drastically reduced transport costs and helped fuel the region's industrial growth. Stretching for 66km, the canal was an essential link in the development of Britain's canal network. It's an important historical landmark and

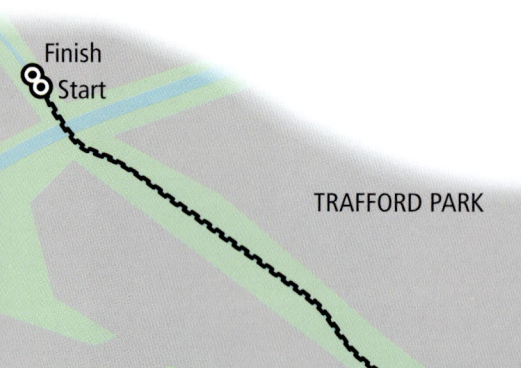

Finish
Start

TRAFFORD PARK

OLD TRAFFORD

ABOVE Trees reflecting in the canal.

its innovative design, featuring tunnels and aqueducts like the Barton Swing Aqueduct, remains an engineering marvel.

## The paddle

Park in the lay-by opposite the Dutton Arms pub. If there are no spaces, there is plenty of off-street parking nearby. Once on the water, head right in a southerly direction. After just 500m you reach the Barton Swing Aqueduct, which gives some stunning views over the Manchester Ship Canal. The swinging action allows larger ships travelling beneath to pass through while allowing smaller vessels to cross above. The bridge is the only swinging aqueduct in the world and was designed by Edward Leader Williams. It opened in 1894 and is still in regular use today. For the next 3km, the canal is lined with trees, obscuring the many industrial estates and factories. At times, it's easy to forget you're paddling through one of England's largest cities.

On your right, the iconic Kellogg's factory is impossible to miss before you reach a T-junction after 4km. Turn left and from here the trees thin out and you start to enjoy the sights of Manchester's tallest skyscrapers in the distance. Another 2km brings you to Manchester United's Old Trafford stadium.

The stadium has stood proud on the banks of the canal since 1910, and with an original capacity of 80,000, it was one of the largest grounds in England. From the stadium it's 3km until you arrive at Giant's Basin, also known as Potato Wharf. This name reflects Manchester's rich history as a centre for the bustling potato trade. After arriving at the basin, you can exit the water along the bank in front of the lock. Cross the bridge towards the Rochdale Canal and enjoy a bite to eat and a refreshing drink at Dukes 92 or Albert's Shed restaurants. Albert's Shed was named after the former owner, who used the building to store his tools. After you are nicely refuelled, it's time to retrace your route back to Eccles.

## Wildlife

Although this is an urban paddle, you can still expect to see swans, Canada geese and mallards.

## Food stops

• The Dutton Arms pub, located at the launch spot, is a great place for a post-paddle drink.
• Dukes 92 and Albert's Shed are located on Castle Street next to the Rochdale Canal, at the turnaround point of the paddle. They have an extensive beer terrace overlooking the canal and offer a modern British menu and a wide selection of beers, wines and spirits.
• If you like street food, then Mackie Mayor is a great place to go – a huge Grade II listed building with over 400 seats. It hosts nine independent kitchens from around the world.

## Getting there

• By car – From the M60, take junction 11 for Eccles on to the A57 Liverpool Road. At the traffic lights immediately before the canal, turn right. The Dutton Arms is 800m on the right.
• By train – The nearest train station is Eccles, situated on the Manchester to Liverpool line. The station is a 10-minute walk to the starting point.
• By bus – The nearest bus stop is Kirkman Avenue. The 10, 33 and 67 buses run regularly from Manchester and Eccles. The bus stop is 100m from the Dutton Arms.

## Other activities

• Chill Factor is the UK's longest indoor real snow ski and snowboard slope. With a main slope of 180m as well as beginner slopes, it is suitable for all abilities.
• The canal towpath runs alongside the canal and is perfect for walking or gentle cycling.
• For fans of one of Britain's favourite soap operas, visit the Coronation Street Experience and discover the story behind life on the street. Explore the set where the show is filmed and take a walk down the famous cobbled street.

## NEED TO KNOW

■ There are no toilet facilities in the lay-by; however, toilets are available in the pub if you buy a drink.

■ A waterways licence is required to paddle on the canal. This can be purchased from the Paddle UK website: paddleuk.org.uk.

ABOVE LEFT Barton Swing Aqueduct.

LEFT Arriving at Potato Wharf.

# HUMBERSIDE

Humberside, nestled in the heart of England's eastern landscapes, offer a unique paddling experience defined by varied waterways, diverse wildlife, and a deep connection to the region's industrial and maritime heritage. With winding rivers, tranquil canals and access to the expansive Humber Estuary, this area is a hidden gem for paddlers seeking to explore both rural and urban environments.

The Lincolnshire Wolds National Landscape adds another layer of charm to the region. Known for its rolling hills, wooded valleys and picturesque villages, it provides a stunning backdrop for outdoor adventures. For paddlers, nearby waterways, such as the River Ancholme, offer serene routes through this idyllic countryside, blending nature and history with every stroke.

The vast waters of the River Humber, one of the UK's great tidal estuaries, dominate the region. Flanked by salt marshes and mudflats, and teeming with birdlife, it makes a paradise for nature enthusiasts. The shifting sands and tidal waters create an ever-changing paddling experience. The iconic Humber Bridge – a marvel of engineering and once the longest single-span suspension bridge in the world – stands as a striking visual landmark for those paddling below.

Whether you're enjoying the calm canals, exploring the tidal reaches of the Humber or seeking adventure on the rivers, Humberside and North Lincolnshire is an ideal destination for paddlers looking to combine nature, history and adventure in an often overlooked part of England. From the rugged beauty of the Humber Estuary to the gentle charm of the Lincolnshire Wolds, this region offers something truly special for all outdoor adventures.

ABOVE Haile Sand Fort.

RIGHT The entrance to Drakeholes canal.

# 39 DRAKEHOLES

The small hamlet of Drakeholes lies on the banks of the rural 74km-long Chesterfield Canal. It is one of the quietest in the canal system and even in peak summer there can be more paddlers than boaters exploring this beautiful waterway. While technically in Nottinghamshire, its location is far enough north, and its paddle route so enjoyable, that it definitely earns its place in this book.

## The Lowdown

**DIFFICULTY** 

**WATER TYPE** Canal

**DISTANCE** 6km (round trip) from tunnel to Gringley Lock. There are options for a much longer paddle

**PARKING** Lay-by

**WHAT3WORDS** ///rafters.importers.cake

**LAUNCH** Canal bankside moorings

## A brief history

The Chesterfield Canal, often known locally as Cuckoo Dyke, was the last waterway to be engineered by James Brindley, 'the father of English canals'. It was designed to transport coal, iron and lead from the resource-rich areas of Derbyshire through to the River Trent, where they were loaded on to larger vessels for wider distribution.

TUNNEL

Start   Finish

ABOVE Gringley Lock.
RIGHT The launch spot at Drakeholes.

The canal's nickname, Cuckoo Dyke, stems from cargo boats called 'cuckoos', a unique type of vessel only found on the Chesterfield Canal. The origins of the name are unknown, and the boats now long gone; however, a replica has recently been built by the Chesterfield Canal Trust and can occasionally be seen cruising along the water.

BELOW Shane inside Drakeholes tunnel.

## The paddle

Park in the lay-by next to the Drakeholes Tunnel picnic area. If this is full, there is another small grass parking area on the opposite side of the road. Go through the gate, passing the picnic tables, and you will see the canal in front of you. Once you are on the water, you have two options.

Paddle 1 If you head right, you'll find yourself winding along this peaceful stretch of canal. This can be a great option if the wind is blowing in any direction. The tree-

lined banks combined with the meandering route ensure that if you do encounter a headwind, you will soon round a bend or return to the cover of the trees. On a clear autumn morning you might even be treated to a breathtaking sunrise. There are 11.5km of uninterrupted serenity before reaching Whitsunday Pie Lock (No 60). About 4km from the start at Drakeholes, you'll come to the village of Clayworth, and another 4km brings you to Hayton village. The Boat Inn pub conveniently sits right next to bridge 66. It's perfect for a mid-paddle rest stop.

**Paddle 2** Launching from the picnic area and heading to the left, then immediately right, you will see the entrance to Drakeholes Tunnel. The tunnel stretches for 135m, and you can clearly see the other end. However, you are recommended to

wear a forward-facing light to enable craft coming the other way to see you. You will notice that the towpath doesn't follow the canal under the tunnel – in the days before the barges had engines, they were 'legged' through. Leggers were canal workers who would lie on top of the boat and push it through the tunnel by 'walking' along the ceiling. Meanwhile, the owner of the boat would lead the pull horses over the hillside and meet up at the other end of the tunnel. Once leaving the tunnel behind, the canal soon bends to the right and then it's a a leisurely 2km until you reach Gringley Lock (No 61). From here, you can return to Drakeholes or continue on, eventually reaching the River Trent.

## Wildlife

Drakeholes sits on the **Chesterfield Canal** and is a Site of Special Scientific Interest. It has also been awarded a prestigious Green Flag award, and is judged to be among the best green spaces in the UK. With its open countryside and tree-lined banks, it is a wonderful spot for encountering a variety of wildlife. Keep your eye out for **kingfishers**, **herons**, **mute swans** and **moorhens**. If you're paddling at dawn or dusk, you might even catch sight of **bats** darting across the water between the trees. For those continuing their paddle, stay alert – you may just spot **toucans** perched nearby, or **apes** swinging from car tyres and hanging on a gazebo! I'll leave it to you to decide if they are real or not.

## Food stops

• **The King William Inn**, Scarforth is an award-winning dog-friendly gastropub with a riverside garden, outdoor bar and pizza shed. It is also dog friendly.
• **The Boat Inn**, located in Hayton next to canal bridge 66, serves traditional pub food with a modern twist. The menu changes with the seasons.

Start

GRINGLEY ON THE HILL

Finish

HAYTON

ABOVE Up early to catch the sunrise at Drakeholes.

## Getting there

• **By car** – From the A1(M), exit at junction 34 and head east towards Bawtry. In Bawtry, continue on the A631 for 6km and turn right to Drakeholes. The lay-by can be clearly seen next to the picnic area.
• **By train** – The nearest train stations are Retford and Gainsborough. Both stations are well connected to the cities of Doncaster and Sheffield.
• **By bus** – There is no bus stop in Drakeholes. The nearest is in Retford, approximately 12km away.

## Other activities

**The Cuckoo Way** stretches the full 74km of the canal towpath, making it an ideal route for walking and cycling. It's the perfect solution for families or groups where not everyone wants to paddle. While some take to the water, others can enjoy the towpath, sharing the journey and creating a memorable day together, each at their own pace.

## NEED TO KNOW

■ A waterways licence is needed to paddle the Chesterfield Canal. This can be obtained from the Paddle UK website: paddleuk.org.uk. Day or week passes can be purchased from the Canal & River Trust.

■ There are no toilet or changing facilities at the lay-by.

# 40 HAILE SAND FORT – CLEETHORPES

**Paddling to Haile Sand Fort is a unique adventure that takes you across the Humber Estuary** to one of Britain's hidden wartime relics. Rising mysteriously from the sea, this concrete and steel sentinel has been standing guard since the First World War. Navigating the shifting tides and open waters, you'll experience the thrill of reaching this isolated and eerie structure with its weathered history and panoramic views of the coast. This is an unforgettable paddle to a once forgotten fortress.

## The Lowdown

**DIFFICULTY** 🌢🌢🌢 depending on conditions

**WATER TYPE** Sea

**DISTANCE** 4km (round trip)

**PARKING** Anthony's Bank car park

**WHAT3WORDS** ///play.scars.pull

**LAUNCH** Beach

## A brief history

Haile Sand Fort and its larger sister, Bull Sand Fort, are two fortifications at the mouth of the Humber Estuary. They were planned in 1914 at the start of the First World War to protect the entrance to the River Humber. Haile Sand Fort was completed in 1917 and stands 18m above the water. Built on a hexagonal base, the four-storey circular reinforced concrete fort was further strengthened with a covering of steel, and was topped with two quick-firing guns. During the Second World War, a steel mesh was constructed between

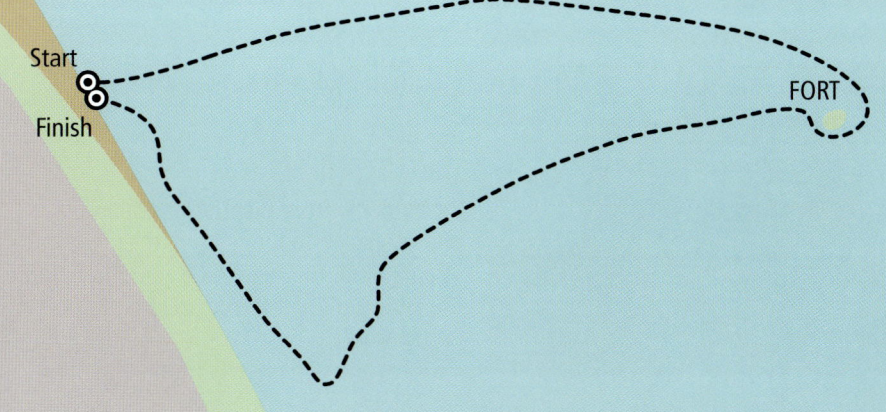

Start
Finish
FORT

the two forts to prevent enemy submarines reaching the ports of Grimsby and Hull. After the war, the fort continued to be manned until the army left in 1956; it then fell into disrepair, and was sold in 2018.

## The paddle

Park in Anthony's Bank car park near the entrance to Cleethorpes Beach Holiday Park and follow the path at the north end that leads to Fitties beach. From the beach you can clearly see Haile Sand Fort, about 1.5km out to sea. In the far distance you can just make out the Bull Sand Fort, further out into the estuary near the shipping lane. The direction to paddle out to the fort is very dependent on the sea state at the time. There are large sandbanks that shift with the currents, so if the water is a little choppy you can get some breaking waves over the sand. Take enough time to stand on the beach and look out at what the water is doing – this will help you pick the best direction. The same applies on your return journey. It can be a good idea to head straight back to shore and paddle back to the start point with the protection of the sandbar providing calm water for the remaining 1km. On other days, the water will be silky smooth all the way to the fort and back, and your route can be as long or short as you desire.

Two kilometres to the east of the beach is the RSPB Tetney Marshes nature reserve. Depending on tides, you can explore the marshes and paddle up Buck Beck until you reach the lock with the Louth Canal. If conditions are not suitable to paddle out to sea, then paddling through the marshes and further along the Louth Navigation is an excellent alternative. Once you have reached the fort you can paddle around it, admire the views and take photos. It can be tempting to scramble up the steps to explore the fort from solid ground, but landing on the structure is prohibited.

## Wildlife

Seals are a common sight around the fort or basking on a sandbank. Porpoises are also seen swimming up and down the estuary. Tetney Marshes is a haven for wetland birds – 70 pairs of redshanks live among the salty marshes and twites and hen harriers can be seen during the winter months.

## Food stops

• At 2.4m x 2.4m (8ft x 8ft), The Signal Box Inn, at Cleethorpes Coast Light Railway declares itself to be the smallest pub on the planet. Selling a good selection of real ales, lagers and ciders from across the country, the pub has a large beer garden just in case it's a little too cosy inside.

• Steels Cornerhouse Restaurant, on Market Street in Cleethorpes, is renowned for its classic fish and chips, a local favourite. It offers a full and diverse menu.

## Getting there

• By car – From Cleethorpes, follow Kingsway on to Kings Road then Anthony's Bank Road. The road takes you through the holiday park and the car park is on the left-hand side.

• By train – The nearest train station is

Cleethorpes, serviced by the TransPennine Express and Northern Rail.
• **By bus** – The 17 bus from Cleethorpes drops off at Cleethorpes Beach Holiday Park (note: at time of writing the timetable still shows Thorpe Park leisure centre), a couple of minutes' walk to the beach.

## Other activities

• **Cleethorpes Coast Light Railway** is a narrow-gauge track running along the Cleethorpes coastline, with various stops along the 6.5km round trip.
• **The Grimsby Fishing Heritage Centre** is an award-winning attraction that transports you back to Grimsby's fishing heyday. The preserved trawler interiors capture the atmosphere of this remarkable and perilous way of life in one of the world's most dangerous occupations.

## NEED TO KNOW

■ Due to the strong currents and shifting sands, it is a good idea to undertake this paddle with a guide or an organised trip. Shane Linford – 'SUP with Shane' – is a local guide with excellent experience of the area.

■ This paddle is best attempted an hour either side of high tide.

■ There are no toilets or changing facilities at the car park.

LEFT Haile Sand Fort (credit Shane Linford)

BELOW Waves breaking over the sandbar.

# BEYOND THE PADDLE

For those looking to explore further, here are some recommendations of books, podcasts, organisations, maps and online resources to deepen your knowledge and enjoyment of all things paddling.

## Books

• **How to Read Water** by Tristan Gooley – Learn to interpret ripples, waves, river patterns and other signs in the natural world to become a more intuitive and observant paddler with this helpful guide.

• **The Secret World of Weather** by Tristan Gooley – A superb companion to *How to Read Water*, this book helps you understand micro-weather patterns. It's ideal for reading skies, clouds and wind shifts and anticipating changes on the water.

• **Invasive Species: A Very Short Introduction** by Dustin J. Welbourne and Julie Lockwood – A compact and informative guide detailing the science of biological invasions in a clear, approachable format. It's great for anyone new to the topic.

• **Recreational Kayaking: The Ultimate Guide** by Ken Whiting – This great all-round instructional book for beginners and intermediate paddlers, covers multiple paddling environments and essential safety techniques.

• **The Paddleboard Bible** by Dave Price – From the basics of getting on and moving, to mastering advanced techniques, this book gives you everything you need to know to get up and get SUPping.

• **Path of the Paddle** by Bill Mason – A classic and beautifully illustrated guide to canoeing techniques, this book covers paddling strokes and philosophy. It's ideal for those who enjoy traditional paddling.

## Podcasts

• **SUPfm Podcast** – This dedicated stand-up paddleboarding podcast features expert guests, technique tips, safety advice, and inspiring paddling stories from across the globe.

• **Rise and Glide** – Discover inspiring conversations from the SUP and watersports community with this podcast.

• **The Adventure Sports** Podcast – This podcast features in-depth interviews covering the lives of sports enthusiasts around the globe.

• **Paddlecast by Paddle UK** – Listen to interviews, stories and tips from across the paddle sports world.

• **The Wild with Chris Morgan** – Though broader in scope, this podcast often touches on rivers, conservation and the natural world.

## Conservation and Access Organisations

• **Paddle UK, www.paddleuk.org.uk** – The national governing body for watersports campaigns for clean, accessible waterways and supports paddle safety.

• **The Rivers Trust, www.theriverstrust.org** – This trust protects and restores UK rivers.

• **Surfers Against Sewage, www.sas.org.uk** – This organisation is active in the campaign for clean water and healthy oceans and rivers.

• **Canal and River Trust, www.canalrivertrust.org.uk** – The mission of this trust is to maintain inland waterways and promote their safe and responsible use.

## Maps, navigation and weather apps

• **OS Maps** – Ideal for in-depth route planning for both inland and coastal waters, this app is great for checking topography and access.

• **Paddle Logger: SUP and Kayaking, paddlelogger.com** – This easy-to-use app allows you to track your paddles, log routes, and enhance safety, with the ability for friends and family to track your movement.

• **Windy App windy.app** – Explore high-resolution wind, wave and weather forecasts on an easy-to-understand map.

• **Met Office Weather App weather. metoffice.gov.uk/weather-app** – Detailed forecasts, rain radar and severe weather warning updates can be found on this app.

• **XCWeather, xcweather.co.uk** – Popular with sailors and wind sport users, this is another great app to use in conjunction with Windy and the Met Office.

• **Tide Times UK, www.tidetimes.co.uk** – This easy-to-use app is perfect for checking daily tide times and heights at hundreds of locations across the UK.

## Online Resources

• **Paddle UK, www.paddleuk.org.uk** – Discover licensing, safety advice, courses and news across the paddling community.

• **Check Clean Dry, www.nonnativespecies.org** – Explore this website to understand and prevent the spread of invasive species while paddling.

• **Freshwater Habitats Trust, www.freshwaterhabitats.org.uk** – Reversing the decline in freshwater biodiversity is the mission of this website.

## Thank You

I'd like to take this opportunity to thank my amazing partner, Karen Greener. This book was always something we planned to do together, so I know how hard it was for you to see me out paddling when injury kept you on the shore. Despite that, you never stopped encouraging me to get out and explore new places. You read every single paddle write-up, patiently fixing my terrible spelling and grammar more times than I can count. Your support, even when it couldn't be on the water, has been behind every page of this book. It still feels like we did this together – because in many ways we did. I could never have finished it without you. I'd also like to thank everyone who has supported this project in both big and small ways – friends, fellow paddlers, local legends, and all those who shared their knowledge, advice and encouragement. Whether you pointed me to a new launch spot, offered safety tips or simply shared stories over an ice cream, your input has helped me enormously. A special thank you to Clara Jump from my publishers, whose help, guidance and endless patience have been invaluable throughout the journey. Most of all, thank you to everyone who loves paddling our beautiful waterways and wants to protect them. This book is for you.

## Final Words

Paddling has a special way of slowing life down. Whether it's a peaceful solo trip or a shared adventure with friends, there's something about being on the water that clears your head and fills your soul. My hope is that this book has helped inspire you to explore new places, paddle safely and appreciate the waterways we are so lucky to have. Whether you're just starting out or have many years of experience, there's always more to discover. Please remember to respect the environment, paddle responsibly, and share your knowledge with others – every small action counts when it comes to keeping our blue spaces clean, safe and accessible for all. Most importantly – enjoy the journey. Happy paddling and see you on the water!

# INDEX